DISMANTLING
the REPUBLIC

DISMANTLING THE REPUBLIC
Copyright © 2017 by Jerry C. Brewer

ALL RIGHTS RESERVED. No part of this publication may be reproduced, distributed, or transmitted in any form or by any means, including photocopying, recording, or other electronic or mechanical methods, or by any information storage and retrieval system without the prior written permission of the publisher, except in the case of very brief quotations embodied in critical reviews and certain other non-commercial uses permitted by copyright law.

Produced in the Republic of South Carolina by

SHOTWELL PUBLISHING, LLC
Post Office Box 2592
Columbia, South Carolina 29202

WWW.SHOTWELLPUBLISHING.COM

Cover Design: Hazel's Dream

ISBN-13: 978-0997939385
ISBN-10: 0997939389

10 9 8 7 6 5 4 3 2 1

Dedication

To the memory of my Great Grandfather

PEYTON G. BREWER (1831-1910)

Pvt., Co. F, 42nd Alabama Infantry Regiment.

A Southern gentleman who was a citizen of, and defended, the last Constitutional government on the North American Continent.

DISMANTLING
the REPUBLIC

Jerry C. Brewer

Foreword by Michael Andrew Grissom

Shotwell Publishing
Columbia, S.C.

Foreword

WHAT PASSES FOR AMERICAN HISTORY today, especially as it pertains to the type of government under which we are now constrained to live, is largely a collection of myths, fables, and legends, which have incrementally supplanted the truth until legend has become the new truth.

Few people, for instance, realize that the republic which was founded in the last few years of the 18th century no longer exists. Nearly everyone today fervently believes that it is still intact, though perhaps battered by the winds of liberalism and its inevitable heir, socialism. Even the popular recent movement called the Tea Party, welcome as it is, clings to the idea that the republic is still with us and is only in need of some fine-tuning. Its well-intentioned leaders and faithful followers, for all their enviable enthusiasm, do not understand that genuine freedom of person and individual liberty, which were commonly held tenets of independence during and immediately following the American Revolution, but which have succumbed to two centuries of political and governmental abuse, cannot be reclaimed simply by lowering taxes, electing Republicans, and fatuously awaiting the ascension to the Presidency of some personality who might—just might—someday appoint a decent, respectable, honest, constitutionalist to the Supreme Court.

What, for instance, does the Tea Party plan to do about a large standing army, ready to invade any country around the world that displeases a sitting President – or worse yet, ready to invade any one of the fifty states which might depart from the "party line?" (Does Arizona come to mind?) Eisenhower sent armed troops into Little Rock, Arkansas, in 1957, when that state displeased him. Kennedy sent 30,000 U.S. Army troops into Oxford, Mississippi, in 1962, when that state displeased him. There is no provision in the U.S. Constitution for a large standing army. Even as late as the War Between the States, Lincoln had to call up volunteers to invade the Southern states; but an ignorant populace believes that the United States has maintained a large "peacetime" army since 1776. Pure legend.

Perhaps the best example of myth and fable is the carefully managed cult figure of Abraham Lincoln. Father Abraham. Not only was Lincoln a scoundrel of the lowest order, admired by many modern-day charlatans, among them Bill Clinton and Obama, he was directly responsible for the deaths of several hundred thousand Southerners, not to mention thousands of Northern soldiers ordered into battle against the South. Yet, the politically correct line, parroted by every school child that goes through twelve years of government schools, is that "Lincoln saved the Union," when in reality, it was Lincoln who destroyed the Union. His mere election caused seven states to withdraw, and his call for volunteers to invade those seven states made four other states—and eventually, parts of two others—to secede. Shot on Good Friday, dying on Easter weekend, just after he had "saved" the Union, gave his cultists the precise propaganda they needed to make him into a Christ figure, and the legend grew until this man, who was not a member of any church, did not attend worship services, nor ever professed a belief in the divinity of Jesus, is now considered one of the great spiritual leaders of the 19th century. Churchgoers regularly hear him quoted in sermons. Legend replacing truth.

And so it is with the state of the republic. In *Dismantling the Republic*, Jerry Brewer strips away fancy and fiction to show us that the republic actually died in 1865. Lincoln spent four years trying to kill it, and it finally succumbed at Appomattox. What we have today has been in the making ever since. Under the withering administrations of Grant and a succession of Union soldiers elected to the Presidency after the War, Franklin Roosevelt and his New Deal, Lyndon Johnson and his Great Society, Bush the elder and his New World Order, Sonny Bush and his eight-year foray into Iraq, Bill Clinton, and then the Marxist Obama, we have arrived at a government that has metamorphosed into something that abuses citizens at home and destroys civilizations abroad. Whatever it is, it is not the republic our Revolutionary patriots gave us, nor what they envisioned. Try as they might to believe the framework of a republic still exists, neo-conservatives and Tea Party activists are deluded. It drew its last breath in 1865, and no amount of rearranging personalities in Congress will bring it back to life. We have to start over, and *Dismantling the Republic* tells us why.

A great misconception that serves to utterly confound people today is the myth that George Washington, whose bronze likeness graces numerous town squares, capitol lawns, and halls of legislation in the South, was an ardent supporter of limited national government and advocate of states' rights. The truth is that Washington, having received his well-earned laurels on the battlefield, was not equipped with that same love of state sovereignty and individual freedom held by many of his contemporaries, such as Patrick Henry, George Mason, and John Randolph. As President, he surrounded himself with ultra-liberals, such as John Marshall and Alexander Hamilton, who worked tirelessly to establish a strong central government. Washington, whose famous quote disavowing political parties, was, nevertheless, an ardent Federalist, opposing great men like Thomas Jefferson and other Anti-Federalists who labored to limit the role of the national government.

Today, most Americans, without realizing it, have transferred their allegiance from the great ideas of the early republic to the mere symbols of the national socialistic government that now exists between our two coasts. It is the flag that people claim to be willing to die for. It is the "Star-Spangled Banner" that must be lustily sung, hand over heart, at every public gathering. It is the sacrosanct image of the U.S. Capitol. The eagle. The military uniform. The colors, red, white, and blue. The Fourth of July. Fireworks. The externals have become the goal, the end result, the aim. They have replaced our noble ideals, our sense of freedom from persecution, our quest to be free, our desire to be independent, our wish to live our lives without interference from government. Symbolism over substance.

So, the question that begs to be answered is: Would the people ever rise-up and eschew the symbols of a government when it becomes detrimental to their freedom? Probably not. The government regularly persecutes Christian churches by disallowing public prayer and display of Christian symbols in public places, refuses to stop the flood of immigrants into this country, levies confiscatory taxes, sends our tax dollars all over the world as "foreign aid," wastes money and lives on unnecessary foreign wars, works overtime criminalizing virtually every aspect of our lives, and discriminates against native-born white Americans in employment, education, and opportunity. Yet, the general public, especially neo-conservatives and Tea Party activists, will, at every opportunity, leap to their feet and recite the Pledge of Allegiance in semi-religious fanatic fervor. If they ever really deliberated on the words of that pledge, they might cease pledging to a government so corrupt and detrimental to their pursuit of liberty and happiness. If they knew who wrote the Pledge and for what reason it was written, perhaps then they might understand that it has actually and deliberately been used against them all these years.

Would Thomas Jefferson or Patrick Henry recognize this thing we still call a republic? To ask is to answer. The old republic is gone. No matter how many symbols we revere, how many parades we conduct, and how many firecrackers we pop on the Fourth of July, we are merely presiding over a corpse. The sooner Americans realize that the better.

Michael Andrew Grissom

Contents

Dedication I

Foreword V

Author's Preface XIII

Chapter 1: "...To Alter Or To Abolish..." 1

Chapter 2: "Free, Sovereign and Independent" 17

Chapter 3: "A More Perfect Union" 24

Chapter 4: Mercantilism and Clashing Cultures 45

Chapter 5: Early Sectional Conflicts 61

Chapter 6: Sovereignty, Secession and Slavery 74

Chapter 7: Toward Final Conflict 85

Chapter 8: An Exercise in State Sovereignty 92

Chapter 9: A Republic of Sovereign States 104

Chapter 10: Lincoln's War on Northern Sovereignty 111

Chapter 11: Lincoln's War on Southern Sovereignty 118

CHAPTER 12: "THE FINAL SOLUTION" 141

CHAPTER 13: ELIMINATING SOVEREIGNTY'S REMNANTS 156

CHAPTER 14: IN THE VALLEY OF DECISION 167

APPENDIX A 183

APPENDIX B 193

ABOUT THE AUTHOR 212

Author's Preface

CONSTITUTIONAL GOVERNMENT in America ended April 9, 1865. It ended four years earlier in the United States with Abraham Lincoln's ascension to the presidency. Within a year of his inauguration, he effectively eliminated Constitutional rights. He suspended the writ of habeas corpus and imprisoned and deported an Ohio Congressman without warrant or due process. He censored telegraphic communications, stopped circulation of newspapers that criticized his autocratic rule and imprisoned many of their editors. He deprived states of representative government, and unilaterally waged war without the consent of Congress by blockading Southern ports and calling for 75,000 volunteers to invade the sovereign States of the South.

The last bulwark of State sovereignty and Constitutional rights in North America, the Confederate States, ceased to exist when Lee surrendered at Appomattox. From that day forward, the Republic of Jefferson, Madison, Mason and Franklin was to be no more. Henceforth, the federal government that was created by sovereign States to be their agent would become their master. All that remained was for the new order of government to dismantle the Republic's remnants.

Individual rights, expressed in State sovereignty, undergirded the Republic. The declaration of those rights by American Colonists in 1776 culminated a centuries-long struggle for recognition of individual sovereignty dating back to the Magna Carta. As Thomas Jefferson expressed it, all men are "endowed by their Creator with certain inalienable rights. Among those are life, liberty, and the pursuit of happiness," and when government fails to protect those rights it is the right of the people to "alter or abolish" that government.

In late spring, 1787, the greatest minds among the American States gathered in Philadelphia to carve out an instrument to strengthen the weaker Articles of Confederation under which they had united in 1777. What they forged was the American Republic—a voluntary union of sovereign States, created by sovereign individuals, and founded upon the Constitution. When their proceedings ended in September a bystander asked Benjamin Franklin what kind of government they had created. He replied, "A republic, if we can keep it." He and the other Founders understood the fragile nature of government—especially their Republic with its delicate balance of powers.

None of the Founding Fathers envisioned a democracy. Their new government was a Republic of Sovereign States with carefully diffused constituencies and Franklin's uneasiness about keeping it was well founded. Even before the Constitution was in its final form, forces were at work to weaken it and institute a government as autocratic as that of George III.

Without surrendering their sovereignty, the States ratified the Constitution, entering into a voluntary compact under it. In so doing, each State reserved for itself the full measure of sovereignty it held before joining the compact, and expressed that in the 10th amendment to the Constitution. State sovereignty meant that any or all of them had the right to freely withdraw from that compact whenever it became destructive of the ends for which it was established.

From the Republic's inception, the sovereignty of its member States suffered erosive political attacks that reached their high-water mark when Lincoln invaded the South and forced seceded States back into the union at bayonet point. Upon his shoulders rests the responsibility for destroying the Republic. But even before the election of 1860, greedy Northern interests were working to change Franklin's Republic into a Consolidated, Mercantile Empire. Lincoln's election culminated those efforts and in the century and a half since his war Lincoln's heirs have almost finished his work. From 1860 until the present, the Republic has been dismantled to such an extent that the Founders would not recognize it if they returned to 21st century America. Their Republic no longer exists. How that came to pass is the thesis we chronicle in this work. The foundation of the American Republic, created by the Constitution of 1787, was the sovereignty of its creator States. From its very beginning efforts were exerted to dismantle the Republic and replace it with a centralized government by incrementally eroding its foundation of State sovereignty—efforts that achieved their goal, for without State sovereignty, that Republic cannot exist.

Governments may control actions, but they cannot control ideas. They may chain a man's body, but they cannot chain his mind. The Republic that Lincoln destroyed first existed as an idea and it still exists in that form. Jefferson Davis said, "The contest is not over, the strife is not ended. It has only entered upon a new and enlarged arena, and the principle for which we contend is bound to reassert itself, though it may be at another time and in another form." Given the grassroots disaffection for the federal social programs being forced upon the states and the arrogant usurpation of Constitutional authority by the federal government today, it appears that the cause of State Sovereignty still reposes in American hearts. Those voices of dissent in Congressional "Town Hall Meetings" and "Tea Parties" across the land in our time are faint sounds from the stirring wings of the great Phoenix of Davis' principle rising from the ashes of Lincoln's war to reassert itself "at another time and in another form."

Deo Vindice!
Jerry C. Brewer
Elk City, Oklahoma

Chapter 1

"...To Alter or To Abolish..."

When, in the course of human events, it becomes necessary for one people to dissolve the political bands which have connected them with another, and to assume among the powers of the earth, the separate and equal station to which the laws of nature and of nature's God entitle them, a decent respect to the opinions of mankind requires that they should declare the causes which impel them to the separation.

We hold these truths to be self-evident, that all men are created equal, that they are endowed by their Creator with certain unalienable rights, that among these are life, liberty and the pursuit of happiness. That to secure these rights, governments are instituted among men, deriving their just powers from the consent of the governed. That whenever any form of government becomes destructive to these ends, it is the right of the people to alter or to abolish it, and to institute new government, laying its foundation on such principles and organizing its powers in such form, as to them shall seem most likely to effect their safety and happiness. Prudence, indeed, will dictate that governments long established should not be changed for light and transient causes; and accordingly all experience hath shown that mankind are more disposed to suffer, while evils are sufferable, than to right themselves by abolishing the forms to which they are accustomed. But when a long train of abuses and usurpations, pursuing invariably the same object evinces a design to reduce them under absolute despotism, it is their right, it is their duty, to throw off such government, and to provide new guards for their future security. Such has been the patient sufferance of these colonies; and such is now the necessity which constrains them to alter their former systems of government.[1]

WHEN THOMAS JEFFERSON WROTE the Declaration of Independence he drew from a large body of thought expressed by political philosophers of the Enlightenment. One of those was John Locke. Born in 1632, Locke authored a work in 1680 entitled *Second Treatise on Government*. In it, he affirmed that man is born as a free sovereign into a state of nature and whatever portion of his individual freedom he delegates to a political society is done voluntarily for the preservation of his greater liberties—that the individual members of political society, not kings, are sovereign.

Whosoever, therefore, out of a state of Nature unite into a community, must be understood to give up all the power necessary for the ends for which they unite into society to the majority of the community, unless they expressly agreed in any number greater than the majority. And this is done by barely agreeing to unite into one political society, which is all the compact that is, or needs be, between the individuals that enter into or make up a commonwealth. And thus, that which begins and actually constitutes any political society is nothing but the consent of any number of freemen capable of majority, to unite and incorporate into such a society. And this is that, and only that, which did or could give beginning to any lawful government in the world.[2]

Locke argued that governments are created by compacts of sovereign individuals who voluntarily associate in commonwealths for the protection of their liberties. From that premise, he concluded that those surrendered freedoms may be reclaimed any time the agent to whom they were surrendered fails in its obligation to protect them. That failure, he said, constitutes a declaration of war upon members of the body politic by the agent of government.

> *. . . whenever the legislators endeavour to take away and destroy the property of the people, or to reduce them to slavery under arbitrary power, they put themselves into a state of war with the people, who are thereupon absolved from any farther obedience, and are left to the common refuge which God hath provided for all men against force and violence. Whensoever, therefore, the legislative shall transgress this fundamental rule of society, and either by ambition, fear, folly, or corruption, endeavour to grasp themselves, or put into the hands of any other, an absolute power over the lives, liberties, and estates of the people, by this breach of trust they forfeit the power the people had put into their hands for quite contrary ends, and it devolves to the people, who have a right to resume their original liberty, and by the establishment of a new legislative (such as they shall think fit), provide for their own safety and security, which is the end for which they are in society.*[3]

The substance of what Jefferson wrote was that the American Colonists were free sovereigns under protection of the English Crown and that the Crown had failed in securing the Colonists' greater rights. The "equality" of which he wrote referred not to the social status of individuals, but to members of political communities who constituted the body politic.

> *That Declaration is to be construed by the circumstances and purposes for which it was made. The communities were declaring their independence; the people of those communities were asserting that no man was born—to use the language of Mr. Jefferson—booted and spurred, to ride over the rest of mankind; that men were created equal—meaning the men of the political community; that there was no divine right to rule; that no man inherited the right to govern; that there were no classes by which power and place descended to families; but that all stations were equally within the grasp of each member of the body politic. These were the great principles they announced; these were the purposes for which they made their declaration; these were the ends to which their enunciation was directed.*[4]

Rule by divine right was an ancient claim among English monarchs and the antithesis of Locke's philosophy. That he had a divine right to rule was boldly affirmed by James I in a speech to parliament on March 21, 1610.

> *The state of monarchy is the supremest thing upon earth; for kings are not only God's lieutenants upon the earth, and sit upon God's throne, but even by God himself they are called gods . . . Kings are justly called gods for that they exercise a manner of resemblance of divine power upon earth, for if you will consider the attributes to God you shall see how they agree in the person of a king. God hath power to create or destroy, make or unmake, at his pleasure; to give life or send death, to judge and be judged not accountable to none; to raise low things and to make high things low at his pleasure; and to God are both soul and body due. And the like power have kings; they make and unmake their subjects; they have power of raising and casting down; of life, and of death, judges over all their subjects, and in all causes, and yet accountable to none but God only. They have power to exalt low things, and abase high things, and make of their subjects like men at chess—a*

pawn to take a bishop or a knight—and cry up or down any of their subjects, as they do their money. And to the king is due both the affection of the soul and the service of the body of his subjects. . .so it is sedition in subjects to dispute what a king may do in the height of his power, but just kings will ever be willing to declare what they will do, if they will not incur the curse of God. I will not be content that my power be disputed upon, but I shall ever be willing to make the reason appear of all my doings, and rule my actions according to my laws.[5]

Sixty-seven years later, the same claim was made by a devout royalist and Justice of the Peace, just three years before Locke wrote the *Second Treatise on Government.*

The laws have not their maintenance from the parliament, as some of the late seditious pamphlets do falsely suggest to the people, but from the king; for it is he that makes judges and justices of the peace and other officers, for the better execution of the laws; and the power of all the forces in this kingdom are in the king, as one of his most just and undoubted prerogatives. . . .And therefore, having jus gladii only in himself, he is both the prime author and preserver of our laws — nay, is no longer a law than the supreme power is pleased to allow it so, because he is uncontrollable in his actions, and hath no lawful superior on earth to control him.

And this power is given him from God, and therefore due to him jure divino; wherefore the king is called by the Apostle, God's officer or minister, not the people's officer; neither doth he bear the sword in vain. And St. Peter strictly chargeth us to submit ourselves to all mankind in authority in regard of the Lord. . . We see then the supreme power lodged in his Majesty jure divina, by the law of God.[6]

Kings' claims of rule by divine right directly clashed with Locke's position that the God-given right to rule inheres in sovereign individuals who constitute the body politic. That was the position of the American Colonies and the claim of any king—George III included—to a "divine right" to rule them was an affront to their sovereignty. Colonial leaders were political products of the Enlightenment who embraced Locke's philosophy of individual sovereignty. Neither Jefferson nor his Colonial contemporaries believed any man was born "booted and spurred" to ride roughshod over members of the body politic as the English kings claimed. The signers of the Declaration of Independence found that claim repulsive but they had no design upon the government of England. Their only purpose was to dissolve their relationship with Britain and govern themselves as sovereigns.

What the British called the Colonies' "rebellion" was something unique in the annals of history. The American Colonies simply declared the dissolution of "the political bands" that bound them to Great Britain and asserted their sovereign right to "assume among the powers of the earth, the separate and equal station to which the laws of nature and of nature's God entitle them." They called for neither abolition of the British monarchy nor the overthrow of Parliament.

American Colonists did not go to war against Britain, nor did the Declaration of Independence include such a declaration. War ensued but it was not precipitated by the Colonists. The failure of the crown to secure the sovereign rights of its people constituted a state of war against them. Their declaration and reclamation of their rights was an act of self-defense. A state of war between the Colonies and Britain already existed before the Colonies declared their independence. Declaring one's independence is not a declaration of war. War is initiated when despots use military force to prevent free people from exercising their God-given rights. American Colonists did not begin the

War for Independence. That war was declared by the British Empire long before 1776.

That the world might know their reasons for declaring independence from Britain, Jefferson enumerated Colonial grievances against the Crown. George III exercised absolute power over them and no law could be enacted by Colonial legislative bodies without his approval. In exercising that power, the king disenfranchised the colonists whom those laws affected.

He has refused his assent to laws, the most wholesome and necessary for the public good.

He has forbidden his governors to pass laws of immediate and pressing importance, unless suspended in their operation till his assent should be obtained; and when so suspended, he has utterly neglected to attend to them.

He has refused to pass other laws for the accommodation of large districts of people, unless those people would relinquish the right of representation in the legislature, a right inestimable to them and formidable to tyrants only.

He has called together legislative bodies at places unusual, uncomfortable, and distant from the depository of their public records, for the sole purpose of fatiguing them into compliance with his measures.

He has dissolved representative houses repeatedly, for opposing with manly firmness his invasions on the rights of the people.

He has refused for a long time, after such dissolutions, to cause others to be elected; whereby the legislative powers, incapable of annihilation, have returned to the

> *people at large for their exercise; the state remaining in the meantime exposed to all dangers of invasion from without, and convulsions within.*
>
> *He has obstructed the administration of justice, by refusing his assent to laws for establishing judiciary powers.*

Of the king's absolute control of judicial processes and the burgeoning bureaucracy sent by him to bleed the Colonies of their resources, Jefferson wrote,

> *He has made judges dependent on his will alone, for the tenure of their offices, and the amount and payment of their salaries.*
>
> *He has erected a multitude of new offices, and sent hither swarms of officers to harass our people, and eat out their substance.*

At the height of Israel's national glory, Solomon wrote, "there is no new thing under the sun"[7] and his observation was borne out with passage of national healthcare legislation in 2010. That measure adds thousands of Internal Revenue Agents to the already bloated federal bureaucracy to "harass our people, and eat out their substance." The more things change, the more they remain the same. Americans today face the same oppressive governmental bureaucracy that their Colonial fathers faced almost two and a half centuries ago.

The next grievance could have been penned this morning. A large standing federal military presence in the States has been the standard practice for decades, including the National Guard which is—in reality—"independent of and superior to civil power" of the States. That will be shown in Chapter Thirteen.

> *He has kept among us, in times of peace, standing armies without the consent of our legislature.*

He has affected to render the military independent of and superior to civil power.

Another of the king's actions toward his American subjects was motivated by his affinity for foreign influences. George III was a German of the House of Hanover and his use of Hessian mercenaries was doubtless influenced by that connection. Foreign influences in domestic law and affairs are strongly resisted and resented by modern Americans. In recent years, some United States Supreme Court Justices have indicated their affinity for "International Law" as a factor in their decisions regarding matters pertaining only to the United States. International law has no place in deciding U. S. Constitutional questions.

Another target of Colonial remonstrance had been a series of laws dubbed "The Intolerable Acts." Those were punitive measures passed by a vengeful Parliament in the wake of the Boston Tea Party. One of the "Intolerable Acts" was a tax on the tea that had been dumped in Boston Harbor in December 1773. "Abolishing the free system of English laws" and "enlarging its boundaries" came in the form of another of the "Intolerable Acts" known as the Quebec Act of 1774. It "provided for the civil government of Canada and extended its boundaries southward to the Ohio River," thereby nullifying all claims of the Thirteen Colonies to the Northwest.[8] Another of the "Intolerable Acts" "in effect annulled the Massachusetts charter."[9]

He has combined with others to subject us to a jurisdiction foreign to our constitution, and unacknowledged by our laws; giving his assent to their acts of pretended legislation:

For quartering large bodies of armed troops among us:

> *For protecting them, by mock trial, from punishment for any murders which they should commit on the inhabitants of these states:*
>
> *For cutting off our trade with all parts of the world:*
>
> *For imposing taxes on us without our consent:*
>
> *For depriving us, in many cases, of the benefits of trial by jury:*
>
> *For transporting us beyond seas to be tried for pretended offenses:*
>
> *For abolishing the free system of English laws in a neighboring province, establishing therein an arbitrary government, and enlarging its boundaries so as to render it at once an example and fit instrument for introducing the same absolute rule in these colonies:*
>
> *For taking away our charters, abolishing our most valuable laws, and altering fundamentally the forms of our governments:*
>
> *For suspending our own legislatures, and declaring themselves to be invested with power to legislate for us in all cases whatsoever.*

Jefferson next catalogued abuses of royal power that endangered the lives of George III's Colonial subjects through a reign of terror by his military.

> *He has abdicated government here, by declaring us out of his protection and waging war against us.*
>
> *He has plundered our seas, ravaged our coasts, burned our towns, and destroyed the lives of our people.*

He is at this time transporting large armies of foreign mercenaries to complete the works of death, desolation and tyranny, already begun with circumstances of cruelty and perfidy scarcely paralleled in the most barbarous ages, and totally unworthy of the head of a civilized nation.

He has constrained our fellow citizens taken captive on the high seas to bear arms against their country, to become the executioners of their friends and brethren, or to fall themselves by their hands.

He has excited domestic insurrections amongst us, and has endeavoured to bring on the inhabitants of our frontiers, the merciless Indian savages, whose known rule of warfare is undistinguished destruction of all ages, sexes and conditions.

This litany of oppressions had been brought to the British government's attention many times before. In October 1774, the First Continental Congress, which denied Parliament's authority and power of taxation over the Colonies, approved a document entitled, "Address to The People of Great Britain." Written by John Jay, who later became a U. S. Supreme Court Chief Justice, the "Address" spelled out their grievances. Jay warned the British people that their government's iron hand of tyranny could be raised against them as it had been against their American brethren and wrote in part,

This being a state of facts, let us beseech you to consider to what end they lead. Admit that the Ministry, by the powers of Britain and the aid of our Roman Catholic neighbors, should be able to carry the point of taxation, and reduce us to a state of perfect humiliation and slavery. Such an enterprise would doubtless make some addition to your national debt which already presses down your liberties and fills you with pensioners and placemen. We presume, also, that your commerce will be somewhat diminished. However, suppose you should prove victorious, in what condition will you then be? What advantages or what laurels will you reap from such a conquest? May not a Ministry with the same armies enslave you? It may be said you will cease to pay them; but remember, the taxes from America, the wealth, and we may add the men, and particularly the Roman Catholics of this vast continent, will then be in the power of your enemies; nor will you have any reason to expect that after making slaves of us, many among us should refuse to assist in reducing you to the same abject state.

Do not treat this as chimerical. Know that in less than half a century the quitrents reserved to the Crown from the numberless grants of this vast continent will pour large streams of wealth into the royal coffers.

And if to this be added the power of taxing America at pleasure, the Crown will be rendered independent of you for supplies, and will possess more treasure than may be necessary to purchase the remains of liberty in your island. In a word, take care that you do not fall into the pit that is preparing for us.

We believe there is yet much virtue, much justice, and much public spirit in the English nation. To that justice we now appeal. You have been told that we are seditious, impatient of government, and desirous of independence. Be assured that these are not facts, but calumnies. Permit us to be as free as yourselves, and we shall ever esteem a union with you to be our greatest glory, and our greatest happiness; we shall ever be ready to contribute all in our power to the welfare of the empire; we shall consider your enemies as our enemies, and your interest as our own.

But if you are determined that your ministers shall wantonly sport with the rights of mankind; if neither the voice of justice, the dictates of the law, the principles of the constitution, or the suggestions of humanity can restrain your hands from shedding human blood in such an impious cause, we must then tell you that we will never submit to be hewers of wood or drawers of water for any ministry or nation in the world.

. . . By the destruction of the trade of Boston the Ministry have endeavored to induce submission to their measures. The like fate may befall us all. We will endeavor, therefore, to live without trade, and recur for subsistence to the fertility and bounty of our native soil, which affords us all the necessaries and some of the conveniences of life. We have suspended our importation from Great Britain and Ireland; and in less than a year's time, unless our grievances should be redressed, shall discontinue our exports to those kingdoms and the West Indies.

It is with the utmost regret, however, that we find ourselves compelled by the overruling principles of self-preservation to adopt measures detrimental in their consequences to numbers of our fellow subjects in Great Britain and Ireland. But we hope that the magnanimity and justice of the British nation will furnish a Parliament of such wisdom, independence, and public spirit as may save the violated rights of the whole empire from the devices of wicked ministers and evil counselors, whether in or out of office, and thereby restore that harmony, friendship, and fraternal affection between all the inhabitants of His Majesty's kingdoms and territories so ardently wished for by every true and honest American.

With their grievances ignored and their lives, liberty, and property jeopardized, the Colonists, turned to their only other alternative—secession from England and establishment of a government that would secure their future liberties. Therefore, as an act of self-defense, Jefferson concluded:

> *In every stage of these oppressions we have petitioned for redress in the most humble terms: our repeated petitions have been answered only by repeated injury. A prince, whose character is thus marked by every act which may define a tyrant, is unfit to be the ruler of a free people.*
>
> *Nor have we been wanting in attention to our British brethren. We have warned them from time to time of attempts by their legislature to extend an unwarrantable jurisdiction over us. We have reminded them of the circumstances of our emigration and settlement here. We have appealed to their native justice and magnanimity, and we have conjured them by the ties of our common kindred to disavow these usurpations, which, would inevitably interrupt our connections and correspondence. We must, therefore, acquiesce in the necessity, which denounces our separation, and hold them, as we hold the rest of mankind, enemies in war, in peace friends.*
>
> *We, therefore, the representatives of the united States of America, in General Congress, assembled, appealing to the Supreme Judge of the world for the rectitude of our intentions, do, in the name, and by the authority of the good people of these colonies, solemnly publish and declare, that these united colonies are, and of right ought to be free and independent states; that they are absolved from all allegiance to the British Crown, and that all political connection between them and the state of Great Britain, is and ought to be totally dissolved; and that as free and independent states, they have full power to levy war, conclude peace, contract alliances,*

establish commerce, and to do all other acts and things which independent states may of right do. And for the support of this declaration, with a firm reliance on the protection of Divine Providence, we mutually pledge to each other our lives, our fortunes and our sacred honour.

Before there ever existed such a thing as a "Government of The United States of America," American Colonial delegates, acted in the capacity of their sovereign States and declared themselves free from the ties that had bound them to Great Britain for nearly two centuries. Separately or in concert, they were now free to chart their own courses as sovereign States among the nations of the world.

---

[1] Declaration of Independence, The Thirteen United States of America.

[2] John Locke, *Second Treatise on Government*, 1690.

[3] *Ibid.*

[4] Jefferson Davis, Farewell Speech to the United States Senate, January 1861.

[5] King James I, "On Monarchy," Speech to Parliament, 21 March 1610.

[6] Sir Peter Leicester's charge to the grand jury at Nether Knotsford, Cheshire, 2 October 1677, *The Stuart Constitution*, ed. J. P. Kenyon (Cambridge University Press: 1987), p. 458.

[7] *Holy Bible*, Ecclesiastes 1:9.

[8] Richard B. Morris, *The Life History of The United States* (Time-Life Books, NY: 1963), vol. 1, p. 154.

[9] *Ibid.*

Chapter 2

"Free, Sovereign and Independent"

His Britannic Majesty acknowledges the said United States, viz: New Hampshire, Massachusetts Bay, Rhode Island and Providence Plantations, Connecticut, New York, New Jersey, Pennsylvania, Delaware, Maryland, Virginia, North Carolina, South Carolina and Georgia to be free, sovereign and independent states; that he treats them as such; and for himself, his heirs and successors, relinquishes all claims to the government, propriety and territorial rights of the same and every part thereof.[1]

THE COLONIES' DECLARATION of Independence from Britain was unparalleled in history, but not surprising given the political philosophies formulated and expounded in the Age of Enlightenment. Political philosophy of that period was rooted in religious thought during the Protestant Reformation that emphasized individual spiritual sovereignty in the priesthood of the believer. In 1520 Martin Luther,

...published and gave wide circulation to three tracts. The first one, An Address To The Christian Nobility of The German Nation, appealed to the German nobles to take a lead in the reformation of the church. The first

part of the tract stated that the pope was hiding behind three walls. The first wall was that the papacy had created a distinction between priest and layman which was not according to Scripture. This placed the spiritual power over the temporal, and in opposition to this Luther asserted "the priesthood of all believers."[2]

Luther asserted the sovereignty of the individual believer, declaring that no earthly priest stood between the believer and God. His principle in the spiritual realm was later adopted by political philosophers. They held that the individual is sovereign in the political realm and born free to pursue life and liberty unfettered by restraints of government—that since the individual derives his rights from God, no king stands between him and the Creator. *Voxpopuli, vox Dei*—"the voice of the people is the voice of God"—was their political creed. Government is derived not from the divine right of kings, but from the God-given rights of the governed. The individual possessing those rights may surrender some of them to the agent of government in order to better secure them, but that does not eliminate his sovereignty in the continued possession of all of his liberty. His rights are, in effect, on loan to the agent who receives them in a fiduciary trust, but he retains the right to recall them when the agent to whom they were surrendered becomes derelict in their protection. That was the position of the men who signed the Declaration of Independence. They asserted their individual sovereignty and the right to form another government when the king violated their inalienable rights derived from God.

The political philosophy of that age had heretofore been only a theory. Now, the American Colonists would translate it into practice. With absolutely no designs on the king or his government, the Americans desired only to go their own ways and govern themselves. But the king was not about to let his milk cow slip away without a fight. The Declaration of Independence was a gauntlet flung at his feet which he would neither abide nor ignore. He immediately placed a bounty on the heads of the Declaration's signers and dispatched troops to North America to bring the "rebellious" Colonies to heel.

Needing a united effort against British aggression, the Continental Congress set about to craft a confederacy of their states. The confederacy they crafted was established under the Articles of Confederation adopted in 1777.

> *The articles of Confederation did not establish a government, but a confederation of sovereign states. The Revolution was being fought to abolish central control, and liberty was deemed safe only when government was sharply restricted and kept close to home where the governed could watch it.[3]*

Five years after declaring their independence from Britain, they secured it with George Washington's victory over Lord Cornwallis' troops at Yorktown and official recognition of their independence came in 1783 in the Treaty of Paris. By that treaty "His Britannic Majesty" acknowledged that the states named in it were "free, sovereign and independent." Each of the original 13 states functioned as a sovereign entity, determining its own destiny, electing its officials, governing its citizens within its own borders, and jealously guarding its hard-won sovereignty. None was willing to surrender its sovereignty to a powerful central government like the one from which they had lately been freed. They knew the dangers of placing their lives and liberty in the hands of another. If that was ever to be, there had to be erected such safeguards that they would never again be subjected to tyranny, and the most powerful buffer against government tyranny was their sovereignty. So long as that was maintained no tyrant could rule them with impunity.

The Treaty of Paris in 1783 clearly recognized the sovereign status of the former colonies. Listing them in Article 1, the treaty said, "His Britannic Majesty" recognized them "to be free, sovereign, and independent states; that he treats them as such...." That Britain negotiated with 13 individual sovereign states—not a central government styled, "The United States of America"—was not only implied, but clearly stated. The American union under the Articles of Confederation in 1777 was undergirded by State sovereignty, as was the Republic ten years later. In neither of those unions did any state surrender its sovereignty to a central power as had been the case under British rule. Britain had created the colonies with sovereignty residing in the British crown, but the States were creators of the unions of 1777 and 1787 with sovereignty residing in each creator State. That was specified in both the Articles of Confederation and the Constitution. Article 1 of the Articles of Confederation said, "The style of this Confederacy shall be The United States of America." In Article 2 they specified that, "Each state retains its freedom, sovereignty, and independence, and every power, jurisdiction, and right, which is not by this confederation expressly delegated to the United States, in Congress assembled."

Their assertion of State sovereignty was later written into the 10th Amendment to United States Constitution in these terms: "The powers not delegated to the United States by the Constitution, nor prohibited by it to the states, are reserved to the states respectively, or to the people." The 10th Amendment is the last of those styled, "The Bill of Rights." These were added to the Constitution when the States insisted that such guarantees be written into it. Among the others enumerated in the Bill of Rights are freedom of speech, freedom of religion and the right of individuals to bear arms.

During the debates on the adoption of the Constitution, its opponents repeatedly charged that the Constitution as drafted would open the way to tyranny by the central government. Fresh in their minds was the memory of the British violation of civil rights before and during the Revolution. They demanded a 'bill of rights' that would spell out the immunities of individual citizens. Several state conventions in their formal ratification of the Constitution asked for such amendments; others ratified the Constitution with the understanding that the amendments would be offered.[4]

That the States insisted on inclusion of a Bill of Rights before they would ratify the Constitution is not surprising. A strong central government without such safeguards could—and probably would—devolve into tyranny. They were not about to surrender their hard-won sovereignty, or even a small portion of it without the guarantee—in writing—that they retained all their rights and privileges not expressly delegated to the United States.

State Sovereignty in The Articles of Confederation

The retention of State sovereignty expressed in the second of The Articles of Confederation was also expressed in other parts of the document. Article 5 mandated delegates to the Congress to be appointed as the legislature of each state decided. Delegates were appointed without a popular vote in their states and could be recalled at any time by the sovereign State they represented. Article 5 said,

> *For the most convenient management of the general interests of the United States, delegates shall be annually appointed in such manner as the legislatures of each State shall direct, to meet in Congress on the first Monday in November, in every year, with a power reserved to each State to recall its delegates, or any of them, at any time within the year, and to send others in their stead for the remainder of the year.*

Nor did the Articles of Confederation allow direct taxes on individuals by the Union they established. Expenses incurred in war time had to be approved by the legislatures of the States, according to Article 8.

> *All charges of war, and all other expenses that shall be incurred for the common defense or general welfare, and allowed by the United States in Congress assembled, shall be defrayed out of a common treasury, which shall be supplied by the several States in proportion to the value of all land within each State, granted or surveyed for any person, as such land and the buildings and improvements thereon shall be estimated according to such mode as the United States in Congress assembled, shall from time to time direct and appoint. The taxes for paying that proportion shall be laid and levied by the authority and direction of the legislatures of the several States within the time agreed upon by the United States in Congress assembled.*

Noticeably absent from the Articles is mention of an executive power. The supreme power of that confederacy was vested in its Congress. That manifested their distrust of power concentrated in the hands of one person and tacitly expressed their sovereign status.

Neither could States with large populations infringe on the sovereignty of the smaller ones by their votes in Congress. Article 5 said, "In determining questions in the United States in Congress assembled, each state shall have one vote." This provision would be revisited when the Constitution of 1787 was written, resulting in the creation of a bicameral federal legislature.

From the sovereignty of the individual, as John Locke explained, came the sovereignty of the state when sovereign individuals convened in deliberations for their mutual good. From that philosophy came the assertion that members of the body politic are "endowed by their Creator with certain inalienable rights" such as "life, liberty, and the pursuit of happiness" and that they have the right to "alter or abolish" their form of government when it fails to maintain those rights. Their unprecedented Declaration in 1776 brought freedom to the thirteen "free, sovereign, and independent" North American States. Out of that came the reassertion of their sovereignty in the Articles of Confederation which would lead to "a more perfect union" ten years later.

---

[1] Article 1, Treaty of Paris, 1783.

[2] F. W. Mattox, Ph. D, *The Eternal Kingdom* (Gospel Light Publishing Co., Delight, Arkansas: 1961), p. 246.

[3] Charles Sellers and Henry May, A *Synopsis of American History* (Rand McNally & Co., Chicago: 1969), p. 60.

[4] http://www.ourdocuments.gov/doc.php?flash=true&doc=13&page=transcript/.

Chapter 3

"A More Perfect Union"

FINDING THE PROPER BALANCE between an effective central power strong enough to govern, but sufficiently restricted to preserve individual liberty, was an ages' old effort. With the age of Enlightenment and the assertion of individual sovereignty, that became even more difficult. To create a government that maintained liberty, but at the same time was strong enough to unify and protect the States was an intellectually herculean task, calling for the greatest minds of the 18th century. The creation of a Republic of Sovereign States under the United States Constitution was born of such minds.

Delegates to the Constitutional Convention—minus Rhode Island—met in Philadelphia from May to September 1787, debating the various issues relating to the document upon which their new government would rest. Paramount among their concerns was the loss of individual rights and State sovereignty. Writing the Constitution was just the beginning. In order for a union to exist under it, nine of those sovereign 13 States had to ratify it to establish it among themselves. That process precipitated numerous debates after the convention through publication of Federalist and Anti-Federalist arguments, and in the ratifying conventions of the several States.

"The series of anti-federalist writings which most nearly paralleled and confronted *The Federalist* was a series of sixteen essays published in the *New York Journal* from October 1787, through April 1788, during the same period *The Federalist* was appearing in New York newspapers, under the pseudonym 'Brutus', in honor of the Roman republican who was one of those who assassinated Julius Caesar, to prevent him from overthrowing the Roman Republic. The essays were widely reprinted and commented on throughout the American states. The author is thought by most scholars to have been Robert Yates, a New York judge, delegate to the Federal Convention, and political ally of anti-federalist New York Governor George Clinton. All of the essays were addressed to 'the Citizens of the State of New York'." [1]

Not surprisingly, the first Anti-Federalist Paper expressed the writer's fear that the new Constitution granted too much power to the central government that would result in negating State sovereignty. That much power, he wrote, is an intoxicant which those possessing it are wont to increase and would do so by consolidating and concentrating it to the detriment of State sovereignty:

> *. . . The legislature of the United States are invested with the great and uncontroulable powers, of laying and collecting taxes, duties, imposts, and excises; of regulating trade, raising and supporting armies, organizing, arming, and disciplining the militia, instituting courts, and other general powers. And are by this clause invested with the power of making all laws, proper and necessary, for carrying all these into execution; and they may so exercise this power as entirely to annihilate all the state governments, and reduce this country to one single government. And if they may do it, it is pretty certain they will; for it will be found that the power retained by individual states, small as it is, will be a clog upon the wheels of the government of the United States; the latter therefore will be naturally inclined to remove it out of the way.*

> *Besides, it is a truth confirmed by the unerring experience of ages, that every man, and every body of men, invested with power, are ever disposed to increase it, and to acquire a superiority over everything that stands in their way. This disposition, which is implanted in human nature, will operate in the federal legislature to lessen and ultimately to subvert the state authority, and having such advantages, will most certainly succeed, if the federal government succeeds at all. It must be very evident then, that what this constitution wants of being a complete consolidation of the several parts of the union into one complete government, possessed of perfect legislative, judicial, and executive powers, to all intents and purposes, it will necessarily acquire in its exercise and operation.[2]*

The ominous warning that, "the power retained by the individual States, small as it is, will be a clog upon the wheels of the government of the United States," and, "the latter therefore will be naturally inclined to remove it out of the way," was prophetic. That is what happened in the ensuing years and continues to the present day. As state sovereignty has been steadily eroded, federal power has grown to dangerous proportions. So before the Constitution was ever ratified there was concern that States would lose their sovereignty to a powerful central government. To allay that concern, Congress proposed amendments to the Constitution that would secure States' and individuals' rights.

> *On September 25, 1789, the First Congress of the United States therefore proposed to the state legislatures 12 amendments to the Constitution that met arguments most frequently advanced against it. . . . Articles 3 to 12, ratified, by three-fourths of the state legislatures, constitute the first 10 amendments to the Constitution, known as the Bill of Rights.[3]*

The Bill of Rights guarantees individual freedoms and State sovereignty. Those rights are, (1) a prohibition against the establishment of a state religion, or prohibiting the free exercise of religion by the people; a guarantee of a free press and the freedom of speech; a guarantee of the people's right to peaceably assemble and petition the government for redress of grievances. (2) A guarantee of the individual's right to keep and bear arms. (3) A prohibition against quartering soldiers in private homes in time of peace without the consent of the owners, or in war except as prescribed by law. (4) A guarantee of one's security in his home against unreasonable searches and seizures, with warrants to be issued only upon probable cause and upon oath, with a particular description of the place to be searched and the persons or things to be seized.

George III had issued search warrants called "Writs of Assistance" to his officers in the Colonies authorizing them to search any person's property for smuggled goods on which British taxes had not been paid. These were general warrants authorizing searches without specifying the search's cause or location of the property to be searched. In 1761 about 60 Boston merchants opposed the writs. They were represented in court by James Otis who argued that "one of the most essential branches of English liberty is the freedom of one's house. A man's house is his castle . . . This writ, if it should be declared legal, would totally annihilate this privilege. Custom-house officers may enter our houses when they please; we are commanded to permit their entry."[4]

(5) A guarantee that, "no person shall be held to answer for a capital, or otherwise infamous crime, unless on a presentment or indictment of a grand jury, except in cases arising in the land or naval forces, or in the militia, when in actual service in time of war or public danger"; a guarantee against double jeopardy. This provides that no person acquitted of a crime may again be

tried for the offense of which he was acquitted; a guarantee against being compelled to testify against oneself in a court of law; a guarantee against deprivation of life or property without due judicial process; and a guarantee that government cannot take private property for public use without compensating the owner. (6) A guarantee of the right to a "speedy and public trial, by an impartial jury of the state and district wherein the crime shall have been committed"; a guarantee of the right of the accused to face his accuser and the witnesses against him; a guarantee of the accused's right to legally summon witnesses to testify in his behalf and the right to legal counsel. (7) A guarantee of the right of trial by jury "in suits at common law, where the value in controversy shall exceed twenty dollars...and no fact tried by a jury, shall otherwise be reexamined in any court of the United States, than according to the rules of common law." (8) A prohibition against excessive bail, excessive fines, and against "cruel and unusual punishment." (9) A guarantee that the rights enumerated in the Constitution "shall not be construed to deny or disparage others retained by the people." (10) A guarantee that the states reserved all powers not specifically delegated to the United States by them in the Constitution. The last two of these amendments are fundamental to maintaining sovereignty. The 9th Amendment guarantees individual sovereignty and the 10th Amendment guarantees state sovereignty

The Bill of Rights has been incrementally attacked for the last 230 years by elitist judges. The extant philosophy of the federal judiciary—especially among recent Supreme Court justices—is that the Constitution is a "living document," subject to change with the times. That means that the intent of its writers has no bearing in our century; that the Constitution means only what the Supreme Court intends it to mean, based upon current culture. This renders the federal judiciary an elitist oligarchy ruling by fiat as a "law unto itself." For instance, the guarantee against a state religion has been "interpreted" by the judiciary to mean that religion cannot be practiced or exercised on certain public property by public officials. That, of course, violates the second clause of the freedom of religion guarantee by "prohibiting the free exercise thereof." This "living document" theory that allows judges to subjectively interpret the Constitution is like the manager of a baseball team interpreting baseball rules during a game. The rules will say whatever he subjectively decides instead of what their writers meant them to say.

Another example is the incessant assault against the 2nd Amendment right to keep and bear arms. It has been argued that this amendment's mention of the militia means the right to bear arms is not individual, but as a collective armed force. Can anyone really believe the Founders thought they had to provide authority in the Constitution for soldiers to carry weapons? That argument is beyond fermented ignorance. The 2nd Amendment is a protective measure for individual and state sovereignty against federal tyranny—not a provision for an army to carry weapons.

Freedom of the press and speech have also come under Congressional attack in recent years. The so-called "fairness doctrine" which has been proposed for broadcasting would effectively silence programming that presents an opposing view to the conventional wisdom of the federal government. The "fairness doctrine" is simply John Adams' "Alien and Sedition Acts" dressed up in modern garb. All of these efforts to destroy our sovereignty can be traced directly to Lincoln's abolition of Constitutional rights in 1861. He opened a "Pandora's Box" of tyranny that paved the way for the complete destruction of Constitutional liberty.

During debates over Constitutional ratification, James Madison explained the compact nature of the Constitution. "Each State, in ratifying the Constitution, is considered as a sovereign body, independent of all others, and only to be bound by its own voluntary act. In this relation, then, the new Constitution will, if established, be a FEDERAL, and not a NATIONAL constitution (*emphasis in the original*)."[5] In Pennsylvania's Ratification Convention, James Wilson, who was a Federalist, said the proposed federal system, "instead of placing the State governments in jeopardy, is founded on their existence. . . . On this principle, its organization depends; it must stand or fall as the State governments are secured or ruined."[6]

A "federal" Constitution meant that the government would be a creation of the States acting in their sovereign capacities. It delegated powers from sovereign States to the federal government and to ensure its federal nature, the Framers deliberated carefully to preserve States' rights in it. The Constitution is a limitation of federal powers, not the States' powers. Sovereignty inheres in the States.

State sovereignty is apparent in the Constitutional provisos for selecting federal officers. No federal official was to be elected in a "democratic vote" of the entire country. A democratic "tyranny of the majority" was as repugnant to the Framers as the tyranny of the British Crown. They were determined that executive, legislative, and judicial power would neither be concentrated in a single branch of government, nor in the "majority" of a democracy. To that end they diffused government powers by separating them into three branches and further diffused them by specifying that each branch would answer to a different constituency. Only in this manner could they safely secure State sovereignty and the liberties of their citizens.

The Federal Legislature

Article I, Section 1 of the Constitution prescribes a bicameral federal legislature: "All legislative powers herein granted shall be vested in a Congress of the United States, which shall consist of a Senate and a House of Representatives." That two legislative houses were prescribed for Congress was a compromise between delegates of the larger and smaller States. Fearing infringement upon their sovereignty by the larger States, the less populous ones insisted on equal representation as had been the case under the Articles of Confederation where each State had a single vote in Congress. Unwilling to give equal representation to the smaller States, the larger ones wanted Congressional representation based upon population. Resulting from this difference was a compromise that created two houses of Congress—the House of Representatives and the Senate. Members of the House of Representatives were to be selected within their States on the basis of their States' populations. The more populous States would have more representatives with more votes than smaller States. On the other hand, the Senate would be composed of two Senators from each State who answered to their respective Legislatures. That gave both large and small States equal representation in the Senate with two votes each.

The House of Representatives would be the forum of the sovereign people within their States and the Senate would be the forum of the sovereign States. This is seen not only in the prescribed manner of selecting members of both houses, but also in their length of terms. Article I, Section 2 says, "The House of Representatives shall be composed of members chosen every second year by the people of the several states and the electors in each state shall have the qualifications requisite for electors of the most numerous branch of the State Legislature." The Representative's constituency consisted of the qualified voters, and he was required to answer to them every two years.

On the other hand, Senators were to represent their sovereign State governments and serve a term of six years. Senators were not to be selected by a popular vote. In each State they would be "chosen by the legislature thereof." They answered to a different constituency than Representatives. Their constituencies were their State Legislatures—not the people at large. The Senate was created to be a powerful restraint against the consolidation of federal power and when Senators spoke in Congress, they spoke as voices of their sovereign State governments. In Massachusetts' Ratification Convention, Fisher Ames said, "The Senators represent the sovereignty of the States. In the other House individuals are represented. . . The Senators are in the quality of ambassadors of the States."[7] In another attack on State sovereignty, that will be considered in another chapter, the method of selecting United States Senators was changed in 1913 by the 17th Amendment to the Constitution.

Ask most school students what the federal separation of powers means and they will say it means there are three branches of government—legislative, executive and judicial. That is true as far as it goes but most modern students are ignorant of the additional diffusion in the constituencies of each branch by the separation of elective powers. That fine distinction is vital to understanding the Framers' intent to preserve State sovereignty.

"The Framers gave the three political components of the federal government (the House, Senate and presidency) different electors (the people, the state legislatures and the Electoral College (as originally intended) to reinforce the principle of separation of powers, by which government is checked and balanced."[8]

The separation of powers with differing constituencies was designed to ensure no individual or branch of government would usurp the power of other federal branches or of the States comprising the Republic.

The Federal Executive

Shortly after the Constitutional delegates convened, Edmund Randolph presented the Virginia Plan on May 29 that proposed a national executive to be elected by the National Legislature. There was mixed reaction to this proposal and on June 1, 2 and 4 the delegates decided upon a single executive who would serve a seven-year term, but be ineligible for re-election. One of the concerns that arose was over the executive's power. Concentrating too much power in the hands of one man was a natural concern considering the absolute power George III wielded over them. Other issues they tackled relating to the executive were his re-eligibility, length of term, and how he would be elected.

Alexander Hamilton—the foremost Federalist and outspoken advocate of a strong central government—proposed a "Governor" as Chief Executive to serve during "good behavior." Under his proposal the "Governor" could serve for life which was tantamount to a monarchy. Hamilton's plan was rejected and through June and July the delegates debated the executive office, agreeing to various other proposals, then revisiting and revising them. A proposal for the executive to be elected by the National Legislature was rejected. With numerous items of the Constitution still at issue, the delegates turned to David S. Brearly of New Jersey to chair a committee that would attempt to resolve those items. One of those was the method of selecting a chief executive for the new government and Brearly's Committee settled on the Electoral College method. The committee's proposal was adopted and written into the Constitution in the following words:

The executive Power shall be vested in a President of the United States of America. He shall hold his Office during the Term of four Years, and together with the

Vice President, chosen for the same term, be elected as follows:

Each State shall appoint in such Manner as the Legislature thereof may direct, a Number of Electors, equal to the whole number of Senators and Representatives to which the State may be entitled in Congress: but no Senator or Representative, or Person holding an Office of Trust or Profit under the United States, shall be appointed an Elector.

The Electors shall meet in their respective States, and vote by Ballot for two Persons, of whom one at least shall not be an inhabitant of the same State with themselves. And they shall make a List of all the Persons voted for, and of the Number of Votes for each; which List they shall sign and certify, and transmit sealed to the Seat of the Government of the United States, directed to the President of the Senate. The President of the Senate shall, in the presence of the Senate and House of Representatives, open all the Certificates, and the Votes shall then be counted. The person having the greatest Number of Votes shall be the President, if such Number be a majority of the whole Number of the Electors appointed; and if there be more than one who have such Majority, and have an equal number of votes, then the House of Representatives shall immediately chuse by ballot one of them for President; and if no Person have a Majority, then from the five highest on the list the said House shall in like Manner chuse the President. But in chusing the President, the Votes shall be taken by States, the Representation from each State having one Vote; A quorum for this purpose shall consist of a Member or Members from two thirds of the States, and a majority of all the States shall be necessary to a Choice. In every case, after the Choice of the President, the Person having the greatest Number of Votes of the Electors shall be the Vice President. But if there should remain two or more who have equal Votes, the Senate shall chuse from them by Ballot the Vice President.[9]

Two items stand out in this provision. First, the president was not to be elected by a popular "democratic" vote. The republican form of government which the Constitution created did not provide for national power to proceed from a particular person or body of that government, but from the States in their sovereign capacities, and the Electoral College would safeguard that sovereignty. Second, the legislatures of the sovereign States were to select presidential electors at their discretion—not the individual voters of those states. Only by authorization of their legislatures were voters permitted to select presidential electors. The Electoral College was designed to prevent a future Absalom from stealing the hearts of the people and usurping State sovereignty in the new Republic.

The Federal Judiciary

The federal judiciary was established by Article III, Section 1 of the Constitution. "The judicial power of the United States shall be vested in one supreme Court, and in such inferior courts as the Congress may from time to time ordain and establish. The Judges, both of the supreme and inferior Courts, shall hold their Offices during good Behaviour, and shall, at stated Times, receive for their Services a Compensation, which shall not be diminished during their Continuance in Office."

Of the three branches of government specified in the Constitution, the judiciary was the most insulated from the people and the other branches of government. Congressional Representatives were elected by voters in their respective districts, Senators were selected by their legislatures, and the president was chosen by Electors selected in a manner authorized by State legislatures. All were selected for specified terms and any of them could be replaced at the discretion of their constituents. But the judiciary was to serve for life and not be amenable to any elective constituency. Federal judges were to be appointed by the federal executive according to Article II, Section 2, which says that the president, "shall nominate and by and with the Advice and Consent of the Senate, shall appoint . . . Judges of the Supreme Court, and all other Officers of the United States, whose Appointments are not herein otherwise provided...." The framers' noble intent to insulate the judiciary from public opinion was the Republic's Achilles heel. Anti-Federalists pointed out the obvious danger inherent in that arrangement before the Constitution was ratified.

This government is a complete system, not only for making, but for executing laws. And the courts of law, which will be constituted by it, are not only to decide upon the constitution and the laws made in pursuance of it, but by officers subordinate to them to execute all their decisions. The real effect of this system of government, will therefore be brought home to the feelings of the people, through the medium of the judicial power. It is, moreover, of great importance, to examine with care the nature and extent of the judicial power, because those who are to be vested with it, are to be placed in a situation altogether unprecedented in a free country. They are to be rendered totally independent, both of the people and the legislature, both with respect to their offices and salaries. No errors they may commit can be corrected by any power above them, if any such power there be, nor can they be removed from office for making ever so many erroneous adjudications. The only causes for which they can be displaced, is, conviction of treason, bribery, and high crimes and misdemeanors. This part of the plan is so modelled, as to authorise the courts, not only to carry into execution the powers expressly given, but where these are wanting or ambiguously expressed, to supply what is wanting by their own decisions.[10]

The legislative and executive branches of the Republic would be subject to removal by their constituencies but that would not be the case with federal judiciary. The Constitution provides for their removal only upon conviction of the crimes enumerated above. The Anti Federalists' concern was well founded. In the last two centuries, the United States Supreme Court has usurped Congressional powers by assuming legislative functions in its "interpretation" of the Constitution. With no Constitutional provision for reversing its decisions, the court's usurpation of legislative prerogatives has vastly diminished State sovereignty in the process, a fear expressed in the Anti Federalist papers.

The opinions of the supreme court, whatever they may be, will have the force of law; because there is no power provided in the constitution, that can correct their errors, or controul their adjudications. From this court there is no appeal. And I conceive the legislature themselves, cannot set aside a judgment of this court, because they are authorised by the constitution to decide in the last resort. The legislature must be controuled by the constitution, and not the constitution by them. They have therefore no more right to set aside any judgment pronounced upon the construction of the constitution, than they have to take from the president, the chief command of the army and navy, and commit it to some other person. The reason is plain; the judicial and executive derive their authority from the same source, that the legislature do theirs; and therefore in all cases, where the constitution does not make the one responsible to, or controulable by the other, they are altogether independent of each other. The judicial power will operate to effect, in the most certain, but yet silent and imperceptible manner, what is evidently the

> *tendency of the constitution: — I mean, an entire subversion of the legislative, executive and judicial powers of the individual states. Every adjudication of the supreme court, on any question that may arise upon the nature and extent of the general government, will affect the limits of the state jurisdiction. In proportion as the former enlarge the exercise of their powers, will that of the latter be restricted.[11]*

George Mason, a Convention delegate from Virginia, is credited, along with James Madison, as being one of the Fathers of The Bill of Rights. Mason feared a federal court having the power of judicial review and warned that such power would destroy State sovereignty.

> *I am greatly mistaken if there be any limitation whatsoever, with respect to the nature and jurisdiction of these courts. If there be any limits, they must be contained in one of the clauses of this section; and I believe, on a dispassionate discussion, it will be found that there is none of any check. All the laws of the United States are paramount to the laws and constitution of any single state. "The judicial power shall extend to all cases in law and equity arising under this Constitution." . . . When we consider the nature of these courts, we must conclude that their effect and operation will be to utterly destroy the state governments, for they will be the judges how far their laws will operate. They are to modify their own courts, and you can make no state law to counteract them. The discrimination between their judicial power, and that of the states, exists, therefore, but in name. . . . For if your state judiciaries are not to be trusted with the administration of common justice, and decision of disputes respecting property between man and man, much less ought the state governments to be trusted with power of legislation. The principle itself goes to the destruction of the legislation of the states, whether or not it was intended. As to my own opinion, I most*

religiously and conscientiously believe that it was intended, though I am not absolutely certain. But I think it will destroy the state governments, whatever may have been the intention. . . . To those who think that one national, consolidated government is best for America, this extensive judicial authority will be agreeable; but I hope there are many in this Convention of a different opinion, and who see their political happiness resting on their state governments.[12]

The Framers of the Constitution labored long with the best intentions to create the Republic, but a single tragic flaw inheres in their work. Supreme Court justices were left without accountability. That has resulted in the enlargement of federal power at the expense of State sovereignty, just as Mason warned in 1788. This flaw provided a latent tool for dismantling the Republic before the Constitution was ever ratified and has been utilized for that purpose for more than two centuries. The first such effort was enacted by the First Congress in 1789.

The Judiciary Act of 1789 specified that the Supreme Court should consist of six justices, that there should be a district court for each state, and that two Supreme Court justices sitting with a district judge should constitute an intermediate court of appeals. The Act also provided for an Attorney General and explicitly specified that any decision in the state courts that questioned federal as opposed to state powers could be appealed to the Supreme Court, thus authorizing the Supreme Court to pass on the constitutionality of state laws.[13]

Since that time, U. S. Supreme Court justices, with neither accountability to a constituency of electors, nor a Constitutional proviso for voiding their decisions, have sat as supreme judges of State laws.

At the Republic's beginning, Sellers and May write that, "both houses [of Congress] were dominated by Federalists."[14] The first Chief Executive, George Washington, favored a strong federal government and appointed arch-Federalist Alexander Hamilton as Secretary of the Treasury. Hamilton's appointment was balanced by Anti Federalist Thomas Jefferson's selection as Washington's Secretary of State. With a Congress dominated by Federalists and a president favoring federalist policies, the new Republic was launched with attempts to consolidate federal power—attempts that would continue until they reached fruition in 1860.

By 1800, the struggle to consolidate federal power through the judiciary was well underway. Federal courts "were staffed entirely by Federalists serving for life, and some of the judges had conducted themselves with egregious partisanship."[15] Federalists who had dominated the government from the beginning were replaced by Anti Federalists in Jefferson's administration who attempted to unravel some of the fabric of central power woven by their predecessors. One of their attempts resulted in the landmark case of judicial review from the Supreme Court of Chief Justice John Marshall in Marbury vs. Madison. Marshall, a Federalist, was an appointee of President John Adams in one of his last acts as Chief Executive. Adams' last days in office saw an expansion of the federal court system, as "President Adams had spent his last hours in office signing commissions for the 'midnight judges' and other officials who were to staff the new courts."[16]

When Jefferson and his Republicans came to power in 1800, they repealed the Judiciary Act and Jefferson instructed "his Secretary of State, James Madison, to withhold the commissions of the Federalists who had been appointed to staff them."[17] Jefferson's order led to the judicial review case of Marbury vs. Madison. On March 3, prior to Jefferson assuming office, "John Marshall, acting as secretary of state, affixed the official seal to the commissions"[18] for the 42 justices of the peace created by the act, but failed to deliver them:

"The next day, after Thomas Jefferson was inaugurated, he directed the new secretary of state, James Madison to withhold delivery of 17 of the 42 commissions, including that of William Marbury. William Marbury sued for a writ of mandamus to require Madison to hand over his commission.

"The decision in Marbury's case, written by Chief Justice John Marshall (the very same John Marshall who affixed the seal to Marbury's commission—talk about a conflict of interest!) established and justified the power of judicial review. It is the first case read by virtually every first-year law student and is generally considered the greatest of all landmark cases. Marshall strained to reach his result. The plain words of Section 13 of the Judiciary Act indicate that Marbury went to the wrong court or invoked the wrong statute (or both), but Marshall proceeded as if the suit were authorized by Section 13 and then declared the statute unconstitutional on the grounds that it purported to expand the Court's original jurisdiction in violation of Article III. Marbury's suit was dismissed for lack of jurisdiction. Marshall's decision—brilliant in its conception—allowed the court to brand Jefferson a violator of civil rights without issuing an order that the President could have ignored."[19]

Marshall's precedent-setting decision, paved the way for further Supreme Court reviews that continue to chip away at State sovereignty. While this case involved a federal legislative act, the precedent was set whereby today's Supreme Court can declare State statutes, such as anti-abortion laws, "unconstitutional," although the Constitution is silent as a tomb on such matters. Marshall's unprecedented review validated the fear expressed in the Anti Federalist Paper, No. 11, which said,

"Every adjudication of the supreme court, on any question that may arise upon the nature and extent of the general government, will affect the limits of the state jurisdiction. In proportion as the former enlarge the exercise of their powers, will that of the latter be restricted." Of Marshall's aim of federal consolidation, Thomas J. DiLorenzo wrote:

> *His career was a crusade to rewrite the Constitution so that it would become a nationalist document that destroyed states' rights and most other limitations on the powers of the centralized state. He essentially declared in Marbury vs. Madison that he, John Marshall, would be the arbiter of constitutionality via "judicial review." The Jeffersonians, meanwhile, had always warned that if the day ever came when the federal government became the sole arbiter of the limits of its own powers, it would soon declare that there were, in fact, no limits on its powers. This of course is what the anti-Jeffersonians wanted—and what has happened.[20]*

That the United States Supreme Court should command such power is analogous to a person charged with a crime deciding his own innocence with no appeal from his decision. Who is to decide whether the Supreme Court has violated the Constitution? Under an insulated federal judiciary, the battle for State sovereignty was joined from the earliest days of the "more perfect union." It would continue to rage for decades until, draped in the mantle of Hamiltonian Federalists, Abraham Lincoln would ascend to power and begin the final dismantling of the American Republic.

---

[1] http://www.constitution.org/afp/brutus01.htm

[2] Anti Federalist No. 1, October 18, 1787. *The Anti-Federalist Papers* (Michigan State University Press, Lansing: 1965).

[3] http://www.freedomhq.com/billofrights.html

[4] http://www.nhinet.org/ccs/docs/writs.html.

[5] *Federalist* No. 39.

[6] The Debates in the Convention of the State of Pennsylvania on the Adoption of the Federal Constitution, Source: http://www.constitution.org/rc/rat_pa.html.

[7] Remarks in the Massachusetts ratifying convention, 19 January 1788, in Jonathan Elliot, *The Debates in the Several State Conventions on the Adoption of the Federal Constitution*, 2:46.

[8] George Will, "Feingold's Vandalism of Constitution," *The Oklahoman,* Feb. 22, 2009, p. 20A.

[9] United States Constitution, Article II, Section 1.

[10] *Anti-Federalist Papers* No. 11, 31 January 1788.

[11] *Ibid.*

[12] "The Debates in the Commonwealth of Virginia, on the Adoption of the Federal Constitution." Source: http://www.constitution.org/rc/rat_va.htm

[13] Sellers and May, *A Synopsis of American History* (Rand McNally & Co., Chicago: 1969), p. 80.

[14] *Ibid.*, p. 79

[15] *Ibid.*

[16] *Ibid.*, p. 92.

[17] *Ibid.*

[18] http://www.law.umkc.edu/faculty/projects/ftrials/conlaw/judicialrev.htm

[19] *Ibid.*

[20] Thomas J. DiLorenzo, "Doomed From The Start: The Myth of Limited Constitutional Government In America," Feb. 25, 2010. Source: http://www.lewrockwell.com/dilorenzo/dilorenzo182.htm

Chapter 4

Mercantilism and Clashing Cultures

ALEXANDER HAMILTON envisioned a much different government than the Framers created in 1787 and he labored mightily to mold theirs into one modeled after British Mercantilism.

"Mercantilism was a system by which the government deliberately controlled the economic affairs of the state ...The ultimate purpose of mercantile policy was to enhance national strength, provide self-sufficiency, and pay for military power. Mercantile theory came to include the notion that no nation could be great without colonies as sources of markets and raw materials."[1]

"To some degree, all of the colonizing powers subscribed to mercantilist notions. To some degree, all mercantilists believed in building self-sufficient national states or empires. . . . Mercantilism implied a dual role for the colonies, whose interests must always be subordinate to the mother country's. First, colonies proved their worth when they furnished products the mother country had previously been compelled to buy from foreign, often enemy, nations. . . . Second, colonies should mean expanding markets for such English goods as cloth, nails and other hardware.

"The English merchant capitalists who invested in colonizing projects believed that their pursuit of profit also served the national welfare."[2]

Hamilton's government, modeled after British Mercantilism, would give rise to sectional conflicts in the 19th century. Protective federal tariffs would reduce Southern States to colonial status to provide raw materials to the "mother country"—the North—while depending on the North for goods formerly obtained at lower cost from England.

The mercantilist blend of state control and private enterprise vastly expanded British influence and created its Empire upon which the sun never set. That was England's formula for colonizing America, and even though Sir Walter Raleigh's Roanoke Colony in 1585 failed, English Mercantilists were undeterred.

"English colonization was still to be a private enterprise, and Raleigh had pointed the way by organizing a 'joint stock company' to finance his second colonial venture. The joint-stock device, a forerunner of the modern corporation, went back to the time of Henry VIII when English merchants had pooled their capital and spread the risks of trade with Russia by buying shares in the 'stock' or capital of the self-governing Muscovy Company. Applied to America, this device not only made English colonization possible, but insured that it would be carried out under the direction of private entrepreneurs seeking private profits as well as national ends."[3]

Mercantilism fueled the Acts of Trade and Navigation, passed by Parliament in the 17th and 18th centuries, to protect British industry against foreign competition. Those acts vastly enhanced the wealth of New England traders and ship builders by stipulating that all goods imported and exported must be in English ships and that the ships' crews must be 75 percent English. That New Englanders were colonists did not affect their businesses. They were English under the protection of those Acts. Mercantilism became so ingrained in the fabric of Colonial society—particularly that of New England—that Hamilton's devotion to it is not surprising.

Infusion of federal funds into the private sector, like the "bailouts" of the banking and auto industries in 2009, is a direct descendant of British Mercantilism advocated by Hamilton. A mutated form of capitalism, mercantilism is, therefore, not capitalism at all. A Mercantile economy is not controlled by the principles of supply and demand as in a purely capitalistic system, but by government regulation and control of private industry. That amounts to a form of socialism and infringes upon the individual's sovereignty in his business, which is what federal regulatory agencies have done since their inception.

One of the pillars of British Mercantilism was the protection of their manufacturers from foreign competition. "Gold and silver would flow into the treasury if the nation sold more abroad than it bought. To ensure such a favorable balance of payments, tariff walls against imports had to be erected, and domestic producers had to be bolstered by ensuring them essential raw materials and low production costs."[4] This centralized government power, favored the wealthy over the poorer classes, and perpetuated aristocracy. Later protection of manufacturers in the United States came through the same kind of restrictive tariffs which amounted to government welfare for the rich. As welfare for the poor has created a dependent underclass in modern society, so corporate welfare—Mercantilism—created a wealthy upper class dependent upon federal subsidies.

Both welfare systems are designed to perpetuate those in power who fund them and in the last 150 years the federal government has pursued both kinds of programs. Corporate welfare was instituted under Lincoln and welfare for the poor under Franklin Roosevelt. That's why the "economy" is considered a major issue in modern elections. Federal parameters prescribed by the Constitution have little meaning to an electorate who love financial security more than their liberties. With the increased growth of a federal welfare/mercantile system has come a corresponding loss of individual liberty and State sovereignty.

Hamilton, the foremost advocate of corporate welfare, presented his views in a speech to the Constitutional Convention by proposing "The British Plan." But his affinity for the British system was not shared by the other Framers and it remained for his ideas to be gradually inculcated into the American political psyche by his later disciples. Hamilton's plan later included the establishment of a national banking system and a corporate welfare system modeled after Britain's. Federal welfare programs for both rich and poor have ballooned to mammoth proportions in the last 150 years, even though the United States Constitution grants none of those powers to any branch of government. Despite lacking Constitutional authority for creating social welfare systems, the federal government has assumed that authority, arguing Hamilton's point that it may do whatever is not Constitutionally prohibited.

At least Hamilton was willing to make what he thought was a reasonable argument. Reason finds no place in the minds of modern politicians who arrogantly brush aside Constitutional arguments about their powers as though their questioners are ignoramuses. A prime example is Congressional House Speakeress, Socialist/Democrat Nancy Pelosi. On October 22, 2009, when questioned about Constitutional authority for Congress' "Health Care Reform" proposal, she brusquely snorted, "Are you serious?"

The struggle between Federalists and Anti Federalists intensified through the first half of the 19th century in the form of a two-party system of government. Republicans (not the modern Republican Party, but Anti Federalists who advocated a federal Republic) were allied against the Federalists (precursors to the Whig and modern Republican parties) in a see-saw struggle for power in the first decades of the 1800s. Anti-Federalists were heirs of Jefferson's view that government, "which governs least governs best," while the Federalists subscribed to Hamilton's concept of a powerful central government founded on British mercantile principles. The clash of those views was a conflict between State sovereignty and federal power that led to the dismantling of the Republic.

Hamilton's first success in implementing his vision for the new Republic came early when another Federalist, George Washington, appointed him as the first Secretary of the Treasury.

"Alexander Hamilton had no sooner taken office than he became the master spirit of the administration; indeed he thought of himself as Washington's prime minister. This remarkable man burned with a vision of national greatness. Aiming at a powerful, unified nation, he detested the localistic tendencies of the states. Convinced that vigorous leadership by the able few, especially in the executive branch of the government, was the only way to build a powerful nation, he feared the turbulence and irresponsibility of the democratic masses. Astutely aware of the relationship between political power and economic power, he was determined to promote the rapid economic growth of the country and to forge firm ties, political and economic, between the government and the wealthy."[5]

Hamilton's greatest achievement in Washington's administration was persuading the Federalist Congress to pass an economic bill establishing a national bank, mandating federal assumption of state debts incurred during the Revolution, increasing tariff rates, and taxing liquor—moves that strengthened federal power over the States. Secretary of State Thomas Jefferson opposed the banking bill. He argued that the "necessary" clause of Section I, Article 8 of the Constitution— empowering Congress "To make all Laws which shall be necessary and proper for carrying into Execution the foregoing Powers and all other Powers vested by this Constitution in the Government of the United States. . . . "—actually prohibited the federal government from establishing a national bank. Jefferson said the word "necessary" was restricted by the 10th Amendment which reserved powers to the States. Washington came down on the side of Hamilton and signed the banking bill into law.

Two other proposals by Hamilton were increases in tariff rates and a direct excise tax on liquor. "He advocated the latter tax frankly on the ground that it would increase the power of the government, and he was especially anxious to have the whiskey-making farmers of . . . the interior feel the power of the federal government directly."[6] The higher tariffs were intended to "give 'infant industries' a competitive advantage in the domestic market until it could become well established."[7]

Hamilton's victory presaged a greater conflict in the coming years. By 1791 a two-party political system that would gravely affect the Republic and lead directly to the loss of State sovereignty was in its embryonic stage in the First Congress. Although in its infancy, the two-party system was operative in the election of 1796. John Adams, running as the Federalists' candidate, was opposed by Thomas Jefferson, representing the Anti Federalists (or Republicans). Adams edged out Jefferson to become the Second President of the United States.

During Adams' administration federalism strongly asserted itself by abridging Constitutional rights. In 1798, Adams, in concert with his Hamiltonian allies in Congress, pressed for and won four measures called the "Alien and Sedition Acts." The

"Sedition" measure was designed to silence administration opponents and prohibited "false, scandalous and malicious writing" against the government. That law unconstitutionally abridged freedom of the press guaranteed in the Bill of Rights.

Responding to the federal government's annulment of a basic Constitutional right, Thomas Jefferson and James Madison authored what were known as the "Kentucky and Virginia Resolutions." Adopted and issued by the legislatures of Kentucky and Virginia, those documents were initial efforts to repeal federal acts that usurped State sovereignty and set the stage for later nullification efforts. Madison, who authored the Virginia Resolution, invoked the 10th Amendment:

> *That the General Assembly doth particularly protest against the palpable and alarming infractions of the Constitution in the two late cases of the 'Alien and Sedition Acts' passed at the last session of Congress; the first of which exercises a power no where delegated to the federal government, and which by uniting legislative and judicial powers to those of executive, subverts the general principles of free government.*
>
> *That this state having by its Convention, which ratified the federal Constitution, expressly declared, that among other essential rights, "the Liberty of Conscience and of the Press cannot be cancelled, abridged, restrained, or modified by any authority of the United States," and from its extreme anxiety to guard these rights from every possible attack of sophistry or ambition, having with the other states, recommended an amendment for that purpose, which amendment was, in due time, annexed to the Constitution; it would mark a reproachable inconsistency, and criminal degeneracy, if an indifference were now shewn, to the most palpable violation of Rights, thus declared, and*

secured; and to the establishment of a precedent which may be fatal to the other.

. . .The General Assembly doth solemnly appeal to the like dispositions of the other states, in confidence that they will concur with this commonwealth in declaring, as it does hereby declare, that the acts aforesaid, are unconstitutional; and that the necessary and proper measures will be taken by each, for cooperating with this state, in maintaining the Authorities, Rights, and Liberties, referred to the States respectively, or to the people."[8]

Invoking its sovereignty, Kentucky followed suit in December 1799 and issued its resolution authored by Thomas Jefferson:

RESOLVED, That this commonwealth considers the federal union, upon the terms and for the purposes specified in the late compact, as conducive to the liberty and happiness of the several states: That it does now unequivocally declare its attachment to the Union, and to that compact, agreeable to its obvious and real intention, and will be among the last to seek its dissolution: That if those who administer the general government be permitted to transgress the limits fixed by that compact, by a total disregard to the special delegations of power therein contained, annihilation of the state governments, and the erection upon their ruins, of a general consolidated government, will be the inevitable consequence: That the principle and construction contended for by sundry of the state legislatures, that the general government is the exclusive judge of the extent of the powers delegated to it, stop nothing short of despotism; since the discretion of those who administer the government, and not the constitution, would be the measure of their powers: That the several States who formed that instrument, being sovereign and independent, have the unquestionable right to judge of its infraction; and that *a nullification, by those sovereignties, of all unauthorized acts done under the colour of that instrument, is the rightful remedy: That this commonwealth does upon the most deliberate reconsideration declare, that the said alien and sedition laws, are in their opinion, palpable violations of the said constitution; and however cheerfully it may be disposed to surrender its opinion to a majority of its sister States in matters of ordinary or doubtful policy, yet, in momentous regulations like the present, which so vitally wound the best rights of the citizen, it would consider a silent acquiescence as highly criminal: That although this commonwealth as a party to the federal compact, will bow to the laws of the Union, yet it does at the same time declare, that it will not now, nor ever hereafter, cease to oppose in a constitutional manner, every attempt from what quarter soever offered, to violate that compact:*

AND FINALLY, in order that no pretexts or arguments may be drawn from a supposed acquiescence on the part of this commonwealth in the constitutionality of those laws, and be thereby used as precedents for similar future violations of federal compact, this commonwealth does now enter against them, its SOLEMN PROTEST.

Approved December 3rd, 1799[9]

It should be noted that while these resolutions were precursors to nullification, they did not outlaw the Alien and Sedition Acts. They merely registered official State protests against them, calling for their repeal. The Kentucky and Virginia Resolutions were the first salvo fired in the battle between sovereign States and federal power that would later erupt in full-fledged nullification by another State. The major point in both resolutions was that the States were sovereign members of a "compact." They had delegated part of their rights to the federal government for protection of the greater portion of them under the Constitution and federal failure to secure those rights constituted a dangerous precedent for further usurpations. State sovereignty had been recognized by Britain in the Treaty of Paris and the States were not about to meekly surrender it to a consolidated federal government engineered by Alexander Hamilton.

Cultural Roots of The Conflict

To gain a better perspective of the conflict between Northern Federalists and Southern Anti Federalists, it is necessary to understand the cultural differences between them. They were two distinct peoples from differing cultural, religious and political backgrounds. There was no political homogeneity between the North and South, and while slavery later became a major issue, it was not the cause of the conflict between them. The cause was a clash of their ancient cultures.

North and the South were both colonized by the English about the same time—Jamestown, Virginia in 1607 and Plymouth in 1620. But subsequent migration into these two sections came in the form of distinctly different British subjects. The Puritans who settled the North were Englishmen who were dissenters from the Church of England. Their purpose was to establish a theocracy in the New World in which they were as intolerant as the Church from which they dissented. They "declined to accept any in the colonies who interpreted the Scriptures differently from themselves. They attempted to make their own Puritanism supreme and exclusive."[10] As Englishmen, the Puritans brought with them a devotion to the British Crown and modeled their society after its absolute power. Empire was their model and to accomplish it in the New World a strong, authoritarian theocracy would be their tool. "The Puritans, who had suffered under the persecution of Archbishop Laud in England, now used similar tactics against opponents in Massachusetts."[11]

To establish their theocracy, the Puritans "emulated other rulers of the time in their abhorrence of democracy, religious toleration and separation of church and state. From the start, the Bay Colony confined voting to members of the approved Puritan churches and denied freedom of speech to its opponents."[12]

Puritanism was a reaction to the moderation of the Anglican Church during the Reformation. In 1527 Henry VIII appealed to Pope Clement VII to set aside his marriage to Catherine of Aragon and allow him to marry Ann Boleyn with whom he was infatuated. Clement refused his petition so Henry took matters into his own hands, broke with the Catholic Church and appointed Thomas Cranmer archbishop of Canterbury in 1533. Cranmer promptly pronounced Henry's marriage to Catherine void and his marriage to Ann Boleyn legal—a marriage which had taken place three months earlier—and in 1534 Henry was made "Supreme Head of The Church of England." This is perhaps the only modern denomination owing its existence to a fornicating king.

The Puritans subscribed to John Calvin's theology, set forth in his work entitled, Institutes of The Christian Religion, published in 1536—two years after Henry became head of the Church of England. Catholicism is a system of "good works" by which supplicants earn their way into heaven. Calvin reacted to this position. He maintained that God is Sovereign, that salvation is by "grace only," that all men are born depraved, that before the world began God elected certain individuals to salvation and the rest to damnation and no works men do can change God's election. Since God elected certain persons to salvation and the rest to damnation, Calvin said the death of

Jesus Christ was only for the elect, leaving the non-elect to their misery and without any hope of eternal salvation. But, according to Calvin, no one knows if he is of the elect unless and until God directly operates upon him in an "experience of grace" which is then subjectively testified to by the recipient.

The earliest English settlers in the Southern Colonies were devout Anglicans and the Church of England flourished in that section. Virginia, known as "The Old Dominion," was so named by Charles I because that Colony remained loyal to him during England's Civil War between Royalists and Puritans. Later migration to the Southern Colonies was by a different people. Vast numbers of those who later settled Virginia and the Carolinas, then migrated to other Southern states, were British subjects but did not consider themselves Englishmen. They were agrarian Celts from Scotland, Wales and Ireland who brought with them the same feelings for the English that the English—especially the Puritans—had for them. About 200,000 Scots migrated to the South between 1704 and 1776, but their relocation to the New World did not magically effect a reconciliation between Celts and the English. Old animosities remained.

Religion was not the only division between North and South. Ancient political animosities remained between them. The Celts had defended their lands and homes against English invaders for centuries. When King Alexander III of Scotland died in 1286, Scottish Lords named Alexander's granddaughter, Margaret, Queen of Scotland. Smelling a political opportunity, Edward I of England arranged for her betrothal to his son, but her death three years later precipitated a struggle for Scotland's crown. In a compromise after Margaret's death, Scottish Lords named John Balliol King but Edward reversed their actions, deposed Balliol and tried him as a felon. Despite pleas from Scottish Lords to respect his promise that Scotland would remain a separate kingdom, Edward invaded Scotland in a war of conquest.

By 1297 the Scots, under the leadership of William Wallace, were defending their land against English invaders. Under Wallace, the Scots routed the Earl of Surrey's forces in a great victory at Stirling on September 11. Less than a year later the tide was turned with an English victory at the Battle of Falkirk and by 1305—three centuries before the Puritans landed at Plymouth—the English had conquered the Scots, captured Wallace and executed him. He was strangled by hanging, but kept alive until he could be disemboweled, emasculated, quartered and beheaded. His head was placed on a pole on London Bridge.

Wallace's fate at English hands paralleled that of Daffydd ap Gruffydd, Prince of Wales, some 22 years before. Prior to his invasion and conquest of Scotland, Edward I had conquered Wales using tactics similar to Lincoln's against the South. Edward's forces plundered the Welsh countryside, destroyed crops and stripped the forests bare. The English captured Welsh Prince Daffyd ap Gruffydd in 1283 and condemned him to a slow agonizing death. He was attached to a horse's tail, dragged through the streets of Shrewsbury, and hanged alive. He was then revived, disemboweled and had his entrails burned before him for his resistance to English power.

The Irish suffered a similar fate. In 1649, 29 years after Plymouth was settled, English Parliamentary troops, commanded by Puritan leader Oliver Cromwell, invaded Ireland, massacred thousands of civilians, and confiscated their lands. Some sources estimate that Cromwell's campaign against the Irish—whom the English regarded as subhuman—resulted in the loss of 15 to 25 percent of Ireland's population through death and exile. Others put the number as high as 50 percent. So far as the Puritans were concerned, Irish Catholics were "heretics" and their war against them was a holy crusade.

In the 1630s, Charles I's and Archbishop of Canterbury William Laud's warm relationship with the Papacy ultimately led to their fall from power. The Puritans revolted in the 1640s and by 1645 Charles was fighting for his throne and Laud was in the Tower of London. With the assumption of Puritan power, the Westminster Assembly abolished the Laudian Prayer Book in January 1645 and on January 10th Laud was executed. Four years later, at the end of the Second English Civil War, Charles I became the first and only English Monarch to be executed. He was beheaded January 30, 1649 by the Puritans who instituted their own brand of religious rule.

Charles I's son, Charles II, was in exile the same year when English Royalists signed a pact with Irish Confederate Catholics allying them with Charles II in his effort to restore the monarchy. Their pact precipitated the Puritans' invasion of Ireland. Cromwell and his Puritan Army were determined to impose their brand of religious absolutism on the Irish that was as oppressive as the English Monarchy. The Puritans considered their imposition of civil and religious rule in Ireland as the work of God—the same theme expressed of the North in Julia Ward Howe's "Battle Hymn of The Republic" during Lincoln's war against Southern State sovereignty.

The English were primarily merchants, conducting their businesses under the protection of British Mercantilism, while the Celts were agrarian. With heavy reliance on the national power to protect their businesses, the Puritans had little use for the agrarian and closely knit culture of the Celts. Celtic society was based on family relations with the clan as the basic unit of government. Each clan was loosely connected with others in the form of tribes with each having its own structure. This arrangement gave wide latitude to the sovereignty of the individual and kept government close to each clan where their liberties could be secured. The English highly regarded societal order and conformity based on class distinctions between nobles and commons, and disdained the liberty loving Celts. English

Puritan attitudes toward, and their treatment of, the Celts paralleled that of the North toward the South and was but a continuation of the ancient cultural dissonance between them.

Conscious or not, the conflicts within the Constitutional Convention of 1787 were expressions of the political and cultural differences between the ancient peoples of Britain—the English who favored national power, and the Celts who valued their sovereign liberty. Those differences later emerged between Northern Federalists and Southern Anti Federalists, whose views were personified in Alexander Hamilton and Thomas Jefferson. That led to intense sectional conflicts until the Celtic South was finally subjected to Northern English power by force of arms.

---

[1] http://www.sagehistory.net/colonial/topics/britishempire.htm#mercantilism

[2] Morris, vol. 1, p. 52.

[3] Sellers and May, p. 5.

[4] Morris, vol. 1, p. 52.

[5] Sellers and May, p. 81.

[6] *Ibid.*, p. 82.

[7] *Ibid.*

[8] James Madison, Virginia Resolutions, 1799.

[9] Thomas Jefferson, Kentucky Resolutions, 1798.

[10] Mattox, pp. 282-283.

[11] Morris, vol. 1, p. 78.

[12] *Ibid.*

Chapter 5

Early Sectional Conflicts

THE FIRST PRESIDENTIAL ELECTION, conducted in 1788, manifested a unity unparalleled in American history. George Washington received every electoral vote cast. That would never again be the case. After the new Republic was launched under the Federalist administrations of Washington and Adams, the Anti Federalist Republicans took the helm of the fledgling ship of State. In the first election in which a two-party system had significance, Anti Federalist Thomas Jefferson received 73 electoral votes to Federalist John Adams' 65 in 1800. Jefferson's Republicans and Adams' Federalists constituted the first political party divide in the country—one that would later crystallize and polarize voters and contribute to the demise of the Republic.

With each branch of the new government vying for supremacy, the Constitution only delayed the outcome of the struggle between Federalists and Anti Federalists. One of the first manifestations of federal executive power was Washington's suppression of the Whiskey Rebellion in 1794. Federal legislative power was flexed during Adams' administration in the Alien and Sedition Acts, followed by John Marshall's assertion of federal judicial power in Marbury vs. Madison. In all of these acts, the States—especially those of the South—saw a federal consolidation of power that threatened their sovereignty.

He must have been a careless reader of our political history who has not observed that, whether under the style of 'United Colonies' or "United States," which was adopted after the Declaration of Independence, whether under the articles of Confederation or the compact of Union, there everywhere appears the distinct assertion of State sovereignty, and nowhere the slightest suggestion of any purpose on the part of the States to consolidate themselves into one body. Will any candid, well-informed man assert that, at any time between 1776 and 1790, a proposition to surrender the sovereignty of the States and merge them in a central government would have had the least possible chance of adoption? Can any historical fact be more demonstrable than that the States did, both in the Confederation and in the Union, retain their sovereignty and independence as distinct communities, voluntarily consenting to federation, but never becoming the fractional parts of a nation? [1]

The momentum that had been building for federal intervention in local enterprise was distilled into the "American System" of Henry Clay in the 1820s. Ostensibly a plan to strengthen and unify the nation, Clay's "American System" was, in reality, a means to further erode State sovereignty. It called for high tariffs, construction of canals and roadways by the federal government—precursors of modern federal and Interstate Highway systems—preservation of the national bank, and maintaining high public land prices. Construction of roads and canals was termed "internal improvements," to be financed by federal revenue generated by the tariffs and land sales.

"Clay was the political heir to Alexander Hamilton and so championed centralized governmental power driven by political patronage for the benefit of what U. S. Senator John Taylor of Virginia called the 'monied aristocracy.' ...Clay spent a large part of his career lobbying for government subsidies for corporations in the name of 'internal improvements.' ...Clay was the fiercest proponent of protectionism in Congress from 1811 until his death in 1852. Northern manufacturers who wanted to be protected from foreign competition with high tariffs made him their man in Congress."[2]

In the early 1800s Henry Clay was the darling of the Whig Party which was determined to create a national empire at the expense of State sovereignty. That determination and resistance to it from Jeffersonian Anti Federalists fueled the sectional controversies that ensued after 1820.

Zealously advocated by Clay and Northern politicians, high federal tariffs had the effect of increasing prices on imported goods. The tariff was a means of artificially raising prices on consumer goods imported from abroad. By imposing high tariffs on importers, the government forced them to raise their prices and pass those costs on to the consumer. This prevented the sale of imported goods at lower prices than those manufactured in the Northern states. The tariff money then went into the national treasury to be expended on "internal improvements"—mainly in the North—and Northern manufacturers relied on the tariffs to protect them against cheaper English goods. Cotton from the South was exported to England where workers labored for much lower wages than those in Northern factories. The South was then forced to buy imported English goods at increased prices because of tariff duties. The agrarian Southern States contended that the tariff was unconstitutional because it bestowed benefits upon one section of the country—the North—that were injurious to them.

The sectional conflicts between North and South were further exacerbated when Congress passed the Tariff of 1828 and John Quincy Adams signed it into law in the last days of his administration. Dubbed the "Tariff of Abominations" by

Southern politicians, they immediately saw it as a two-edged sword that would shred their economy. Not only did the Tariff—with rates as high as 45 percent—create higher prices for Southern consumers, but it resulted in England reducing the amount of cotton they imported from the South, which further crippled the Southern economy.

The Tariff of Abominations was the spark that ignited the Nullification controversy, led by Vice-President John C. Calhoun and Senator Robert Y. Hayne of South Carolina. In a document entitled "Exposition and Protest," South Carolina set forth its remonstrance against the tariff much like the Kentucky and Virginia resolutions had done in 1798 and 1799. Calhoun penned the document anonymously, as had Jefferson in the Kentucky Resolutions. In its rough draft he wrote:

> *That the manufacturing States, even in their own opinion, bear no share of the burden of the Tariff in reality, we may infer with the greatest certainty from their conduct. The fact that they urgently demand an increase, and consider every addition as a blessing, and a failure to obtain one as a curse, is the strongest confession that, whatever burden it imposes, in reality falls, not on them, but on others. Men ask not for burdens, but for benefits. The tax paid by duties on imports, by which, with the exception of the receipts from the sale of the public lands, and a few incidental items, the Government is wholly supported, and which, in its gross amount, annually equals about $23,000,000, is then, in truth, no tax on them. Whatsoever portion of it they advance as consumers of the articles on which it is imposed, returns to them with usurious interest through an artfully contrived system.*[3]

As an "artfully contrived system" of the Northern combine of politicians and manufacturers, the Tariff of Abominations was viewed by Calhoun and other Southern politicians as another step in the relentless erosion of State sovereignty by legislation that usurped Constitutional powers.

> *"In order to have a full and clear conception of our institutions, it will be proper to remark that there is, in our system, a striking distinction between Government and Sovereignty. The separate governments of the several States are vested in their Legislative, Executive, and Judicial Departments; while the sovereignty resides in the people of the States respectively. The powers of the General Government are also vested in its Legislative, Executive, and Judicial Departments, while the sovereignty resides in the people of the several States who created it. But, by an express provision of the Constitution, it may be amended or changed by three-fourths of the States; and thus each State, by assenting to the Constitution with this provision, has modified its original right as a sovereign, of making its individual consent necessary to any change in its political condition; and, by becoming a member of the Union, has placed this important power in the hands of three-fourths of the States—in whom the highest power known to the Constitution actually resides. Not the least portion of this high sovereign authority resides in Congress, or any of the departments of the General Government. They are but creatures of the Constitution, and are appointed but to execute its provisions; and, therefore, any attempt by all, or any of these departments, to exercise any power which, in its consequences, may alter the nature of the instrument, or change the condition of the parties to it, would be an act of usurpation.*[4]

Set forth in eight points, the final draft of the Exposition and Protest was much shorter than the rough draft and somewhat milder in its tone when the South Carolina Legislature approved it. But it echoed the primary objection to the consequences of the

Tariff of Abominations—it was unconstitutional and violated State sovereignty.

The Senate and House of Representatives of South Carolina, now met and sitting in General Assembly, through the Hon. William Smith and the Hon. Robert Y. Hayne, their Representatives in the Senate of the United States, do, in the name and on behalf of the good people of the said Commonwealth, solemnly protest against the system of protecting duties, lately adopted by the Federal Government, for the following reasons:

1st. Because the good people of this commonwealth believe, that the powers of Congress were delegated to it, in trust for the accomplishment of certain specified objects which limit and control them, and that every exercise of them, for any other purposes, is a violation of the Constitution as unwarrantable as the undisguised assumption of substantive, independent powers not granted, or expressly withheld.

2d. Because the power to lay duties on imports is, and in its very nature can be, only a means of effecting objects specified by the Constitution; since no free government, and least of all a government of enumerated powers, can, of right, impose any tax, any more than a penalty, which is not at once justified by public necessity and clearly within the scope and purview of the social compact; and since the right of confining appropriations of the public money to such legitimate and constitutional objects is as essential to the liberties of the people, as their unquestionable privilege to be taxed only by their own consent.

3d. Because they believe that the Tariff Law passed by Congress at its last session, and all other acts of which the principal object is the protection of manufactures, or any other branch of domestic industry, if they be considered as the exercise of a supposed power in

Congress to tax the people at its own good will and pleasure, and to apply the money raised to objects not specified in the Constitution, is a violation of these fundamental principles, a breach of a well-defined trust, and a perversion of the high powers vested in the Federal Government for federal purposes only.

4th. Because such acts, considered in the light of a regulation of commerce, are equally liable to objection— since, although the power to regulate commerce, may like other powers be exercised so as to protect domestic manufactures, yet it is clearly distinguishable from a power to do so, eo nomine, both in the nature of the thing and in the common acceptation of the terms; and because the confounding of them would lead to the most extravagant results, since the encouragement of domestic industry implies an absolute control over all the interests, resources, and pursuits of a people, and is inconsistent with the idea of any other than a simple, consolidated government.

5th. Because, from the contemporaneous exposition of the Constitution in the numbers of the Federalist (which is cited only because the Supreme Court has recognized its authority), it is clear that the power to regulate commerce was considered by the Convention as only incidentally connected with the encouragement of agriculture and manufactures; and because the power of laying imposts and duties on imports, was not understood to justify, in any case, a prohibition of foreign commodities, except as a means of extending commerce, by coercing foreign nations to a fair reciprocity in their intercourse with us, or for some other bona fide commercial purpose.

6th. Because, whilst the power to protect manufactures is nowhere expressly granted to Congress, nor can be considered as necessary and proper to carry into effect any specified power, it seems to be expressly reserved to the States, by the tenth section of the first article of the Constitution.

7th. Because, even admitting Congress to have a constitutional right to protect manufactures by the imposition of duties or by regulations of commerce, designed principally for that purpose, yet a Tariff, of which the operation is grossly unequal and oppressive, is such an abuse of power, as is incompatible with the principles of a free government and the great ends of civil society—justice, and equality of rights and protection.

8th. Finally, because South Carolina, from her climate, situation, and peculiar institutions, is, and must ever continue to be, wholly dependent upon agriculture and commerce, not only for her prosperity, but for her very existence as a State—because the valuable products of her soil—the blessings by which Divine Providence seems to have designed to compensate for the great disadvantages under which she suffers in other respects—are among the very few that can be cultivated with any profit by slave labor—and if, by the loss of her foreign commerce, these products should be confined to an inadequate market, the fate of this fertile State would be poverty and utter desolation; her citizens, in despair, would emigrate to more fortunate regions, and the whole frame and constitution of her civil polity, be impaired and deranged, if not dissolved entirely.

Deeply impressed with these considerations, the representatives of the good people of this commonwealth, anxiously desiring to live in peace with their fellow-citizens and to do all that in them lies to preserve and perpetuate the union of the States and the liberties of which it is the surest pledge—but feeling it to be their bounden duty to expose and resist all encroachments upon the true spirit of the Constitution, lest an apparent acquiescence in the system of protecting duties should be drawn into precedent—do, in the name of the commonwealth of South Carolina, claim to enter upon the journals of the Senate, their protest against it as unconstitutional, oppressive, and unjust.

Which exposition is fully submitted

J. Gregg, Chairman
December, 19, 1828 [5]

Passage of the Tariff of 1828 set the stage for another battle between federal power and State sovereignty in the Nullification Crisis that ensued four years later. Southern objections to the Tariff of Abominations resulted in a compromise tariff act, passed and signed into law by President Andrew Jackson on July 14, 1832. The latter was intended to reduce tariff rates imposed in 1828, but the reductions were not enough for South Carolinians. In November, South Carolina called a convention to nullify the tariff as unconstitutional and abusive of State sovereignty. That resulted in passage of the Nullification Ordinance. Citing the passage of the Tariff Acts of 1828 and 1832, the ordinance said the tariffs were, "unauthorized by the constitution of the United States, and violate the true meaning and intent thereof and are null, void, and no law, nor binding upon this state, its officers or citizens..."[6]

Angered by the constant flow of mandates from Washington, a number of states have enacted resolutions in recent years to remind the federal government of the 10th Amendment which reserves undelegated powers to the States. Among those are Oklahoma, Texas and Tennessee. Upset by unfunded federal mandates and the 2009 bailouts of the auto and banking industries, the Oklahoma Legislature passed a Joint Resolution asserting and affirming that State's sovereignty. A Joint Resolution required the signature of Democrat Governor Brad Henry, but he refused to sign it, saying the resolution obligated the state to return funds it had received from the federal government. The legislature then bypassed the requirement for Henry's signature by adopting a Concurrent Resolution which said in part, "That the State of Oklahoma hereby claims sovereignty under the Tenth Amendment to the Constitution of the United States over all powers not otherwise enumerated and granted to the federal government by the Constitution of the United States." Like that of Texas, Oklahoma's resolution was forwarded to the office of the President of the United States, the United Sates Congress and to the State's Congressional delegations. With the erosion of State sovereignty in the last 148 years, these resolutions may be too little, too late. None has the force of law, but they are reminders to the federal government that it is a creation of the states, not their creator.

Another modern State went even further in asserting its sovereignty. On April 15, 2009, Montana Governor Brian Schweitzer signed into law a bill exempting firearms, firearms accessories, and ammunition manufactured and retained in that state from federal regulation under the Commerce Clause of the Constitution. The Montana law cites the 10th Amendment as authority for its enactment and says, "The guaranty of those powers is a matter of contract between the state and the people of Montana and the United States as of the time that compact with the United States was agreed upon and adopted by Montana and the United States in 1889."[7]

When Tennessee passed a similar law to Montana's, federal bureaucrats demonstrated their animosity toward state sovereignty by threatening Tennessee gun manufacturers. The Assistant Director of the federal Bureau of Alcohol, Tobacco, Firearms and Explosives, Carson W. Carroll, told Tennessee that the federal government has a right to regulate their firearms even if those items remain in the state.

The major difference between Montana's law and South Carolina's Nullification Ordinance is that Montana did not nullify a federal law. It simply asserted its sovereignty by exempting from federal regulation firearms manufactured, sold and retained in the State of Montana. South Carolina not only asserted her sovereignty by nullifying the Tariffs in that State, but served notice that if coercive action came from the federal power in Washington, she would dissolve her connection with the union "and will forthwith proceed to organize a separate government, and do all other acts and things which sovereign and independent states may of right do."[8]

President Andrew Jackson reacted to South Carolina's ordinance by instructing the customhouse officer at Charleston to collect the duties and, in the first real act of the War Between The States, sent an armed vessel to enforce his order. Jackson, a Southerner, slave holder, and a Federalist, argued in his *Proclamation To The People of South Carolina* that the union cannot be broken and no State has the right to secede. While conceding the reserved powers under the 10th Amendment, Jackson split hairs, saying, the United States "is a government in which all the people are represented, which operates directly on the people individually, not upon the States; they retained all the power they did not grant. But each State having expressly parted with so many powers as to constitute jointly with other States, a single nation, cannot from that period, possess any right to secede."[9]

Jackson's words portended more federal intervention in the decades to come by his dictum that the Constitution formed a "single nation" operating directly upon the people of the States. It appears that by 1832 the American Republic, whose officers had differing constituencies and whose powers were vastly diluted thereby, no longer existed in the minds of politicians like Jackson. He proclaimed a single, consolidated government wherein States not only delegated certain powers to the federal government, but in so doing surrendered all of their sovereignty. Arguing that even if the union was formed by a compact, that compact is a "binding obligation" which prohibits secession, Jackson ignored the fact that a compact is broken when one of the parties to it fails to fulfill its "binding obligation." That was South Carolina's point. When the federal government fails in securing State sovereignty the compact is broken before secession. In that case, federal failure has already severed its relationship with a State. Jackson's argument would later be transformed into the socialist propaganda phrase, "One nation indivisible" that school children are required to regurgitate each day.

In the wake of the Nullification Ordinance, a compromise was drafted, but not before Congress passed the Force Bill in February 1833, authorizing the president to use force against South Carolina—another portent of the clash to come. At the same time this measure passed, another tariff bill was enacted that was acceptable to South Carolina and that state repealed its Nullification Ordinance in March 1833. The crisis had been averted and the sectional conflict temporarily subsided.

---

[1] Davis, Introduction to *The Rise and Fall of the Confederate Government*.

[2] Thomas J. DiLorenzo, *The Real Lincoln* (Three Rivers Press, NY: 2003) pp. 62-63.

[3] Rough Draft, "Exposition and Protest." Source: http://oll.libertyfund.org.

[4] *Ibid.*

[5] "Exposition and Protest of the South Carolina Legislature." Source: http://oll.libertyfund.org

[6] South Carolina Nullification Ordinance, Nov. 24, 1832.

[7] Montana State Legislature, House Bill No. 246, signed into law April 15, 2009.

[8] South Carolina Nullification Ordinance.

[9] President Andrew Jackson, *Proclamation To The People of South Carolina*, Dec. 10, 1832.

Chapter 6

Sovereignty, Secession and Slavery

FROM 1787 TO 1860 the outcome of the struggle between Federalists and Anti Federalists hung in the balance. Central to the issue was State sovereignty and whether States voluntarily entering the union could exercise a Constitutional right to leave it. Andrew Jackson said they could not, but the matter was far from settled, nor has it ever been legally settled in a court of law. The issues of State sovereignty and secession are inseparable. As sovereigns, the States have the right to choose their own courses and that includes secession. On the other hand, if secession is not an option for them, then they are no longer sovereign.

State sovereignty was the Polar Star of the Republic's existence. The union was a creation of the States, not their creator, and it was the settled conviction of the best political thinkers in the Republic that when freely formed compacts between States become destructive of men's rights, the people of those States have the sovereign right to withdraw and form another. That right was expressed by Jefferson when he wrote, "Whenever any form of government becomes destructive to the ends for which it was established, it is the right of the people to alter or abolish it, and to institute new government." Even Abraham Lincoln was a secessionist in his early years before lust for national power rendered him duplicitous. As a Congressman in 1847, he stated on the floor of the House of Representatives that, "Any people, anywhere, being inclined and having the power, have the right to rise up and shake off the existing government, and form a new one that suits them better." Secession was not viewed as treason. It was a sovereign right inherent in the people of any State and a right which was exercised by the American Colonies when they seceded from Britain in 1776.

When secession is mentioned, the departure of Southern States from the union in 1861 generally comes to mind. But secession had been often threatened in the Republic from its earliest years and the first threats to secede came not from the South, but from New England States. President John Adams' Secretary of State, Timothy Pickering of Massachusetts, led such a movement in 1802, and in 1844 William Lloyd Garrison, publisher of the abolitionist paper, *The Liberator,* called for secession. Some New England States did secede from the union, after a fashion, during the War of 1812.

"...the New England governors refused to supply troops, and by December 1814, a convention of the New England states met at Hartford to seek redress against the tyranny of the federal government. Some participants advocated the secession of New England, but the more moderate majority contented itself with proposing constitutional amendments that would protect the interests of their section." [1]

As a political philosophy, secession was taught in the United States Military Academy at West Point in the early 1800s. Cadets studied from a standard textbook entitled, *A View of the Constitution,* written by William Rawle and first published in 1825. In his book, Rawle advocated the Constitutional right of any State to secede from the union. Ironically, Rawle was a Quaker and an ardent abolitionist. As a Quaker, he eschewed violence and during the American Revolution he fled to London and studied law.

Rawle, who was born in Philadelphia April 28, 1759, and died April 12, 1836, established his law practice in 1783 in Philadelphia. When George Washington became the Republic's first president, he appointed Rawle as the United States district attorney for Pennsylvania in 1791. It was in that capacity that Rawle prosecuted leaders of the Whiskey Rebellion in 1794.

Article IV., Section 4 of the Constitution says, "The United States shall guarantee to every State in this Union a Republican Form of Government, and shall protect each of them against Invasion; and on Application of the Legislature, or of the Executive (when the Legislature cannot be convened), against domestic Violence." This section was the object of Rawle's remarks in Chapter 34 of his book in which he said, "The Union is an association of the people of republics; its preservation is calculated to depend on the preservation of those republics."[2] Rawle said the federal power is authorized by this section to maintain (guarantee) such form of government in each member State of the union by force, if necessary. Then, without qualification, he wrote,

> *Yet it is not to be understood, that its interposition would be justifiable, if the people of a state should retire from the Union, whether they adopted another or retained the same form of government, or if they should, with the express intention of seceding, expunge the representative system from their code, and thereby incapacitate themselves from concurring according to the mode now prescribed, in the choice of certain public officers of the United States.*[3]

Rawle's point was that a representative form of government is not necessary in order to be a republic but to remain a member of the union a State must have a representative government.

From that, he concluded that secession from the Union is an absolute right of State sovereignty.

> *It depends on the state itself to retain or abolish the principle of representation, because it depends on itself whether it will continue a member of the Union (emphasis added). To deny this right would be inconsistent with the principle on which all our political systems are founded, which is, that the people have in all cases, a right to determine how they will be governed.*

> *This right must be considered as an ingredient in the original composition of the general government, which, though not expressed, was mutually understood, and the doctrine heretofore presented to the reader in regard to the indefeasible nature of personal allegiance, is so far qualified in respect to allegiance to the United States. It was observed that it was competent for a state to make a compact with its citizens, that the reciprocal obligations of protection and allegiance might cease on certain events; and it was further observed, that allegiance would necessarily cease on the dissolution of the society to which it was due.*

> *The states, then, may wholly withdraw from the Union, but while they continue, they must retain the character of representative republics.*[4]

Rawle said a State's Constitutional right to secede is because "the people have in all cases, a right to determine how they will be governed." A State must maintain a representative form of government to remain in the Union, but Rawle said that form of government may be abolished because each State has a right to determine "whether it will continue a member of the Union. "Thus is joined the right to abolish representative government with the corollary right of secession. Pointing out that the rights of secession and dissolution of representative government were understood by the Founding Fathers from the beginning of the Republic and that a state's allegiance to the union would cease at secession, he concluded that States, "may wholly withdraw from the Union." That was the standard political philosophy taught to West Point cadets in the early 1800s, and each of them—including those who later became Union generals—understood a State's right to secede from the union. If secession is "treason," then "treason" was taught to its future military officers at West Point by the United States government.

Rawle's principles were cited by Mississippi's United States Senator, Jefferson Davis, when he resigned from that body after his State seceded in 1861. Davis, a West Point graduate, hero of the Mexican War, and former Secretary of War under President Franklin Pierce, lectured his colleagues on State sovereignty and explained the difference between secession and nullification.

> *I hope none who hear me will confound this expression of mine with the advocacy of the right of a State to remain in the Union, and to disregard its constitutional obligation by the nullification of the law. Such is not my theory. Nullification and secession, so often confounded, are, indeed, antagonistic principles. Nullification is a remedy which it is sought to apply within the Union, against the agent of the States. It is only to be justified when the agent has violated his constitutional obligations, and a State, assuming to judge for itself, denies the right of the agent thus to act, and appeals to the other states of the Union for a decision; but, when the States themselves and when the people of the States have so acted as to convince us that they will not regard our constitutional rights, then, and then for the first time, arises the doctrine of secession in its practical application.*

Secession belongs to a different class of remedies. It is to be justified upon the basis that the states are sovereign. There was a time when none denied it. I hope the time may come again when a better comprehension of the theory of our Government, and the inalienable rights of the people of the States, will prevent any one from denying that each State is a sovereign, and thus may reclaim the grants which it has made to any agent whomsoever.

...It is by this confounding of nullification and secession that the name of a great man whose ashes now mingle with his mother earth has been invoked to justify coercion against a seceded State. The phrase, "to execute the laws," was an expression which General Jackson applied to the case of a State refusing to obey the laws while yet a member of the Union. That is not the case which is now presented. The laws are to be executed over the United States, and upon the people of the United States. They have no relation to any foreign country. It is a perversion of terms—at least, it is a great misapprehension of the case—which cites that expression for application to a State which has withdrawn from the Union. You may make war on a foreign state. If it be the purpose of gentlemen, they may make war against a State which has withdrawn from the Union; but there are no laws of the United States to be executed within the limits of a seceded State.[5]

Davis referred to the Nullification Ordinance passed by South Carolina in 1832 and Andrew Jackson's reaction to it. Jackson had said he was obligated "to execute the laws" of the United States against South Carolina. Davis conceded that point, based upon the fact that South Carolina was a member of the union, but told his colleagues that United States law is not applicable within a State which has withdrawn from the union. He delineated the difference between South Carolina in 1832 and Mississippi in 1861 and restated Rawle's doctrine that the States were sovereign and entitled to enter or leave the union at the will of their people.

Agitation Against Slavery

The abolitionist movements that sprang up in the North in the early 1800s had their roots in two distinct sources—religion and politics. In a case of history repeating itself, the source of abolitionist agitation in the early 1800s and the so-called "civil rights movement" of the 1960s was Northern religion. Discarding any spiritual concern for eternal salvation, Northern churches became wholly secularized in both movements and remain so to this day. Their emphasis on the world to come was long ago removed and their efforts were shifted to propagating the social/political gospel of the here and now.

The irony in Northern abolitionist movements is that they came from the same people who made their fortunes in the slave trade. Not a single slave was brought from Africa to North America in Southern ships. The slave trade was a staple of New England for more than a century before it was outlawed. Those same New England slave traders who sold Africans to Southern planters told those planters a few years later that slavery was wrong and demanded Southerners free the slaves they had sold them. As Confederate Major General D. H. Hill said, a Yankee "repents of everybody's sins except his own." Most people know that New Englanders provided slaves to the South, but few are aware of slavery's unusual legal origin in America.

"In 1650, there were only 300 negroes in Virginia, about one percent of an estimated 30,000 population. They were not slaves, any more than were the approximately four thousand white indentured 'servants' working out their loans for passage money to Virginia, and who were granted 50 acres each when freed from their indentures, so they could raise their own tobacco.

"Slavery was established in 1654 when Anthony Johnson, Northampton County, convinced the court that he was entitled to the lifetime services of John Casor, a negro. This was the first judicial approval of life servitude, except as punishment for a crime.

"But who was Anthony Johnson, winner of this epoch-making decision? Anthony Johnson was a negro himself, one of the original twenty brought to Jamestown (1619) and 'sold' to the colonists. By 1623, he had earned his freedom and by 1651 was prosperous enough to import five 'servants' of his own, for which he received a grant of 250 acres as 'headrights.'

"Anthony Johnson ought to be in the 'Book of Firsts.' As the most ambitious of the first 20, he could have been the first negro to set foot on Virginia soil. He was Virginia's first free negro and first to establish a negro community, the first negro landowner, the first negro slave owner and as the first, white or black, to secure slave status for a servant, he was actually the founder of slavery in Virginia. A remarkable man." 6

Modern revisionists claim abolitionist agitation in the 1800s was a moral crusade and the single cause of the War Between The States. But the earliest conflicts over slavery were neither religious nor moral. They were political.

"Sectional issues appear conspicuously in the debates of the Convention which framed the Federal Constitution, and its many compromises were designed to secure an equilibrium between the sections, and to preserve the interests as well as the liberties of the several States. African servitude at that time was not confined to a section, but was numerically greater in the South than in the North, with a tendency to its continuance in the former and cessation in the latter. It therefore thus early presents itself as a disturbing element, and the provisions of the Constitution, which were known to be necessary for its adoption, bound all the States to recognize and protect that species of property. When at a subsequent period there arose in the Northern States an antislavery agitation, it was a harmless and scarcely noticed movement until political demagogues seized upon it as a means to acquire power. Had it been left to pseudo-philanthropists and fanatics, most zealous where least informed, it never could have shaken the foundations of the Union and have incited one section to carry fire and sword into the other."[7]

It wasn't until later that Northerners took up the cause of emancipation on the basis of religious and moral scruples, intensifying the conflict between the two sections. The strength of the abolitionist groups that sprang up in the early 1800s steadily increased in the 1840s and 1850s, prodded by fiery Northern Protestant evangelists. Northern religion was in a state of flux and great revivals were conducted appealing to the emotional instincts of those who attended. Sellers and May call this "Romantic Christianity," which they define as an assumption "that the world was designed for man's happiness and . . . emphasized man's ability . . . Romanticism was a reaction against the Enlightenment's mechanical view of the natural world and its emphasis on intellect."[8] Romanticism heavily influenced 19th century religion and was the major factor in its rejection of spiritual concerns for an emphasis on material existence and social justice. This thought later evolved into the social gospel of the 20th century that is now a nigh universal tenet of American Protestantism.

"Under the impact of the eighteenth-century Enlightenment, some members of the more sophisticated classes had abandoned the inscrutable, omnipresent God of the Calvinists for Deism's more remote and kindly Creator. . . coming to believe that a reasonable God was favorably disposed toward all men, that men were sufficiently endowed with reason to be capable of goodness, and that the objective of a religious life ought to be goodness in this world rather than God's arbitrary salvation in a world to come."9

By de-emphasizing the spiritual and embracing Romanticism, 19th century Northern religion positioned itself for a purely social agenda and laid the groundwork for Humanism and a secular American society in the 20th century. Though they had religious scruples against slavery, abolitionists had no scruples at all about the means to achieve their ends—not even murder. Such a person was John Brown. He and his sons terrorized Eastern Kansas and massacred Southerners at Pottawatomie in 1856. Brown, who was later captured and hanged, was typical of violent abolitionists who believed the end justifies the means, even at the cost of State sovereignty and human life. Yet for all its posturing and opposition to slavery, religious abolitionism did not achieve its aim until after 1860—and then only by unconstitutional means that destroyed State sovereignty.

---

[1] Sellers and May, 101.

[2] William Rawle, *A View of The Constitution*, 1825, Chapter 34.

[3] *Ibid.*

[4] *Ibid.*

[5] Jefferson Davis, Farewell Speech to the United States Senate, January 1861.

[6] WPA Writers' Program, *Virginia, Guide to the Old Dominion* (Oxford Univ. Press: NY, 1940), p. 378.

[7] Jefferson Davis, Preface to *The Rise and Fall*. . . .

[8] Sellers and May, pp. 146-147.

[9] *Ibid.*, pp. 148-149.

Chapter 7

Toward Final Conflict

THE SWELLING TIDE of issues that carried the States toward final conflict can be classified under two headings—state sovereignty and economics. The conflict that ensued from 1861 to 1865 was the final struggle for sovereignty of the States against a powerful empire envisioned by Northern industrialists who were determined to eradicate the Republic.

The issues of State sovereignty and economics were conjoined. All others relating to that final conflict rest under one or both of those headings as manifested in newspaper editorials in both the North and South during that period.

> *Why is it that the South is perfectly willing for the North to secede, while the reverse is not true of the North as respects the South? There must be a reason for this, as there is for everything else and the reason is plain enough . . . They know that the South is the main prop and support of the federal system . . . They know that it is the [Southern States'] import trade that draws from the people's pockets $60 million or $70 million per annum in the shape of duties, to be expended mainly in the North and in protection and encouragement of Northern interests . . . They know that they can plunder and pillage the South, as long as they are in the same Union with us. . . . They are enraged at the prospect of being spoiled of the rich feast upon which they have so*

long fed and fattened, and which they were just getting ready to enjoy with still greater [relish] and gusto.[1]

Southern newspapers were not the only ones addressing economic concerns of the States. Northern editors intoned the same theme. In a February 19, 1861 editorial, The Manchester, New Hampshire *Union Democrat* said, "The Southern Confederacy will not employ our ships or buy our goods. What is our shipping without it? Literally nothing. The transportation of cotton and its fabric employs more ships than all other trade. It is very clear that we must not let the South go." *The New York Times* chanted the same mantra on March 30, 1861. "With us it is no longer an abstract question—one of Constitutional construction, or of the reserved or delegated power of the State or Federal Government, but of material existence and moral position both at home and abroad . . . We were divided and confused until our pockets were touched." Even foreign papers recognized that economic issues divided the North and South:

> *The grievances which to the South seemed so intolerable that civil war {sic} itself was a lighter evil, were two (one was actual, the other was, in the main, hypothetical). They were suffering, and had long suffered, from the effects of the various Northern Tariffs; and they believed from past experience that as soon as the North had the power in its hands they should be exposed to the same perilous dealing with their slaves . . . But it is clear that the first reason is the one on which the South mainly acted. The proof is very simple. Secession was an absolute and immediate remedy for the free-trade grievance . . . The protective system had been won as a triumph by the North . . . The South felt the double sting of humiliation and of loss. They felt that they were wronged. And it did not seem likely that the evil would abate of itself in the course of time; the wants of the Treasury were growing, and as those wants grew, the tariff was likely to rise.*[2]

The 'Tariff' question, again, enters largely (more largely than is commonly supposed) into the irritated and aggrieved feelings of the Southerners. And it cannot be denied that in this matter they have both a serious injury and an unconstitutional injustice to resent ... All Northern products are now protected; and the Morill [sic] Tariff is a very masterpiece of folly and injustice. No wonder that the citizens of the seceding States should feel for half a century they have sacrificed to enhance the wealth and profits of the North and should conclude, after much futile remonstrance, that only in secession could they hope to find redress.[3]

In an 1849 speech, Senator John C. Calhoun of South Carolina warned of the economic danger to States by federal redistribution of wealth. Subsequent history has proven Calhoun's words to be prophetic:

The two, disbursement and taxation, constitute the fiscal action of the government. What one takes from the community in the name of taxes is transferred to the portion of the community who are the recipients under that of disbursements ... The necessary result, then, of the unequal fiscal action of the government is to divide the community into two great classes, one consisting of those who, in reality, pay the taxes and, of course, bear exclusively the burden of supporting the government; and the other, of those who are then the recipients of their proceeds through disbursements, and who are, in fact, supported by the government, or in fewer words, divide it into tax-payers and tax-consumers.[4]

Calhoun referred to the tariffs that took money from the South to be expended in the North, but he accurately described the federal welfare system for the "poor" that began in the 1930s and continues more than three quarters of a century later. Beginning with Franklin Roosevelt's policies in 1933, the modern Democrat/Socialist party—the antithesis of Southern Democrats of the 19th century—created a dependent underclass of welfare recipients by which it has largely perpetuated itself in power. While one class of Americans—"the tax-payers"—supports the fiscal wants of the federal government, another class—the "tax-consumer"—receives this money in the form of "entitlements."

According to the English historian Thomas B. Macaulay:

> *A democracy cannot survive as a permanent form of government. It can last only until its citizens discover that they can vote themselves largesse from the public treasury. From that moment on, the majority (who vote) will vote for the candidates promising the greatest benefits from the public purse, with the result that a democracy will always collapse from loose fiscal policies, always followed by a dictatorship.*[5]

The loose fiscal policies of the federal government in the last 75 years have led America down the road to ruin with deficit spending and a growing national debt of astronomical proportions. Not only is the welfare underclass promised security from the cradle to the grave, but the federal government now provides a safety net for corporations such as the auto and banking industries—the modern mercantile legacy of Hamilton, Clay, and Lincoln. Both rich and poor have become "tax-consumers" in this modern egalitarian democracy that carries the seeds of its own destruction.

The Issue of Slavery

With a near unanimous voice, modern historians insist that the War Between The States was fought over the single issue of slavery. In that insistence, they stereotype all Southern slave holders as racists and, in the finest tradition of Salem witch hunters, maintain their absolute righteousness as accusers and the absolute depravity of the Southern accused. Their broad brush paints every former slave holder as a sadistic fiend intent upon punishing and/or destroying the Negro. That revisionist myth has been swallowed whole by a mentally sedated, politically correct, intellectually bovine society that has been dumbed down by a century of public school brainwashing.

In 1850, my Great-Great Grandmother, Sarah Hickman Brewer, purchased a Negro girl, named "Clary," for $600.00 in Alabama. To assert that she purchased Clary at such a large sum solely to mistreat or injure her is beyond asininity. That's analogous to buying a new automobile today, driving it home and beating it with a sledge hammer. Slaves were valuable property and were protected as such. Citing the exceptions of abusive slave owners, Harriet Beecher Stowe in *Uncle Tom's Cabin* and Alex Haley in *Roots* stereotyped all slave owners as sadists—propaganda that has become the conventional wisdom of modern academia. While abuses of slaves did occur, it is neither fair nor "scholarly" to brand all slave owners as Stowe and Haley portrayed them. Using like generalities, one could as easily argue that marriage should be outlawed since some husbands abuse their wives.

As an economic factor, slavery was an issue in the ultimate conflict between North and South, but it was by no means the cause of that conflict. Slaves were property in slave holding States, in which millions of dollars were invested. Emancipation—as Lincoln proclaimed—deprived slave holders of their property without due process of law or recompense for their value.

Northern abolitionist agitation over slavery had its roots among the Quakers whose views eventually spread to other religious groups. Given the widespread racism in the North, abolitionists at first found little support for their cause. But as the early decades of the 19th century passed, their support grew in proportion to the North's intense disdain for Southern political power. The abolitionists' cause was a corollary to the deep seated and ancient hatred of Celtic culture that was rooted in the English North, and in the end, became the *cause celebre* of Union politicians—not as a moral or religious cause, but as one to achieve political ends. The South's agrarian economy was built on the institution of slavery. The destruction of that economy with its political power was the sole aim of Northern politicians and to accomplish that they embraced abolitionism.

Nor was abolition exclusively a Northern cause. Abolitionist societies had existed in the South before they did in the North and many Southerners—both slave owner and non-slave owner—had wrestled with the problem of their "peculiar institution." Robert E. Lee freed his slaves long before the War Between The States, and Stonewall Jackson owned no slaves. Years earlier Thomas Jefferson had addressed the slavery issue in the same vein. Missouri and Maine were admitted to the union in 1820—the former as a slave State and the latter as a free State—as a compromise to maintain the balance between the two. Jefferson said that compromise was only a temporary answer to the slavery issue for which no easy solution could be found.

> *But this is a reprieve only, not a final sentence. A geographical line coinciding with a marked principle, moral and political, once conceived and held up to the angry passions of men, will never be obliterated; and every new irritation will mark it deeper and deeper. I can say with conscious truth that there is not a man on earth who would sacrifice more than I would, to relieve us from this heavy reproach, in any practicable way. The cession of that property, for so it is misnamed, is a bagatelle which would not cost me in a second thought, if, in that way, a general emancipation and expatriation could be effected, and gradually, with due sacrifices, I*

think it might be. But, as it is, we have a wolf by the ear, and we can neither hold him, nor safely let him go. Justice is in one scale, and self-preservation in the other.[6]

Jefferson was astute in two observations—that the compromise admitting Maine and Missouri to the Union would not be the final word on the slave issue, and that slavery placed Americans in an untenable position like a man holding a wolf by the ear. Like many of his fellow Southerners, Jefferson also expressed the hope that slavery would be eliminated by gradual emancipation and "expatriation."

---

[1] Editorial, *New Orleans Daily Crescent*, January, 1861.

[2] *The Quarterly Review*, London, 1861.

[3] *The Northern British Review*, Edinburgh, 1862.

[4] John C. Calhoun, "A Disquisition on Government," 1849.

[5] Lord Thomas B. Macaulay, Letter To An American Friend, May 23, 1857.

[6] Thomas Jefferson, Letter to former Maine Senator, John Holmes, April 20, 1820.

Chapter 8

An Exercise in State Sovereignty

ABRAHAM LINCOLN personified every trait opposed to the Republic founded upon the Constitution of 1787. Allied with Northern industrial interests, his opportunistic political career began with his election to the Illinois legislature in 1834 as a member of the Whig Party. Following reelection to a second term in 1836, he became the Whigs' House Leader. As a Whig, Lincoln was enamored with Henry Clay and his American System which advocated protectionist tariffs for industry and federal spending on "internal improvements" such as canals and railroads, and a national banking system. When Clay opposed James K. Polk for the presidency in 1844, Lincoln stumped for Clay in Illinois and spoke against the annexation of Texas as an extension of slavery. In 1846 Lincoln won a seat in the United States House of Representatives as a Whig and remained in that party until 1854 when the passage of the Kansas-Nebraska Act divided it. The Kansas-Nebraska Act opened the new territories to slavery and was opposed by Northern Whigs. When the new Republican Party was formed in a convention at Jackson, Michigan, on July 6, 1854 Northern Whigs defected to it. Thus began the modern Republican Party that sprang from Clay's Whigs.

A powerful central government, based upon tenets of Hamiltonian Federalism undergirded the Republican Party and its founding tolled the death knell for State sovereignty. With their sectional party controlled by Northern industrialists,

Republicans would consolidate their power for the next six years and bring the seething conflict between North and South to a head.

Southern suspicions of Northern interference in State sovereignty were further aggravated in 1859 by John Brown's raid on the federal arsenal at Harper's Ferry, Virginia. Brown, the fanatical abolitionist who butchered Southerners in Kansas, had seized guns and ammunition at the arsenal to arm his followers for a slave revolt in the South. United States Marines, under the command of Robert E. Lee, assaulted the arsenal and captured Brown who was later hanged for his crime. Brown's attempt to incite slave insurrections greatly alarmed Southerners. Their suspicions of a Northern conspiracy were further heightened when they discovered Brown's scheme had the financial backing of prominent and wealthy Northern Republican abolitionists.

With Brown's raid still fresh in their memory, the South was further alienated when Lincoln received the Republican nomination for the presidency in 1860. Southern political power was diminished even more that year when Democrats split into Northern and Southern factions and two other political parties nominated candidates. Illinois Senator Stephen A. Douglas was nominated by the Northern Democrats and Southern Democrats nominated John C. Breckenridge of Kentucky. A fourth party to field a candidate —the Constitutional Union Party—nominated John Bell of Tennessee. That four-way race sealed the doom of Southern political power as Lincoln swept every Northern state. Breckinridge carried the South, with Douglas and Bell garnering but three or four states' electoral votes. The Electoral College majority in the Northern states assured Lincoln of the presidency with only a plurality of popular votes cast. Lincoln received 1,865,908 popular votes which was only 39.8 percent of the total, but the Northern electoral votes sealed his victory.

Douglas garnered 1,380,201 popular votes for 29.5 percent. Breckinridge received 848,019 popular votes for 18.1 percent of the total cast and 72 electoral votes, while Bell came in dead last with 590,901 popular votes—12.6 percent of the total—and 39 electoral votes. Receiving just over a third of the total votes cast, Abraham Lincoln became the nation's 16th President.

In his first inaugural address Lincoln demonstrated his lifelong devotion to the American System of his idol, Henry Clay, and his Orwellian ambitions. His speech was based entirely on Clay's Compromise Speech of 1850, President Andrew Jackson's Proclamation against the Nullification Ordinance, and arch-Federalist Daniel Webster's reply to South Carolina Senator Robert Hayne in their Senate debate on States' Rights. Webster had maintained that the union was older than the Constitution and as it was "perpetual" no state could secede from it. By the time Lincoln was inaugurated seven States had already seceded from that "perpetual union" and his inaugural speech portended dark things to come for those who had left the union.

> *I hold that in contemplation of universal law, and of the Constitution, the Union of these States is perpetual. Perpetuity is implied, if not expressed, in the fundamental law of all national governments. It is safe to assert that no government proper, ever had a provision in its organic law for its own termination. Continue to execute all the express provisions of our national Constitution, and the Union will endure forever—it being impossible to destroy it, except by some action not provided for in the instrument itself.*
>
> *Again, if the United States be not a government proper, but an association of States in the nature of a contract merely, can it, as a contract, be peaceably unmade, by less than all the parties who made it? One party to a contract may violate it—break it, so to speak, but does it not require all to lawfully rescind it?*

Descending from these general principles, we find the proposition that, in legal contemplation, the Union is perpetual, confirmed by the history of the Union itself. The Union is much older than the Constitution. It was formed in fact, by the Articles of Association in 1774. It was matured and continued by the Declaration of Independence in 1776. It was further matured and the faith of all the then thirteen States expressly plighted and engaged that it should be perpetual, by the Articles of Confederation in 1778. And finally, in 1787, one of the declared objects for ordaining and establishing the Constitution was, "to form a more perfect Union." But if destruction of the Union, by one, or by a part only, of the States, be lawfully possible, the Union is less than perfect than before the Constitution, having lost the vital element of perpetuity.

It follows from these views that no State, upon its own mere motion, can lawfully get out of the Union, — that resolves and ordinances to that effect are legally void, and that acts of violence, within any State or States, against the authority of the United States, are insurrectionary or revolutionary, according to circumstances.

I therefore consider that in view of the Constitution and the laws, the Union is unbroken; and to the extent of my ability I shall take care, as the Constitution itself expressly enjoins upon me, that the laws of the Union be faithfully executed in all the States. Doing this I deem to be only a simple duty on my part; and I shall perform it, so far as practicable, unless my rightful masters, the American people, shall withhold the requisite means, or in some authoritative manner, direct the contrary. I trust this will not be regarded as a menace, but only as the declared purpose of the Union that will constitutionally defend and maintain itself.[1]

From his premise of "perpetual union" Lincoln concluded that the seven seceded States were still in the union under federal jurisdiction and their action was "insurrectionary or revolutionary," despite the absence of any "insurrectionary or revolutionary" language from their secession ordinances. No seceding State advocated the overthrow of the union, as none of the Colonies had advocated the overthrow of the British government in 1776. But Lincoln was a masterful political wordsmith and his sentiments—ominously portending bloodshed—were applauded by Northern Republicans.

The election and inauguration of a president by a sectional party committed to their destruction was the straw that broke the camel's back for Southern States and lit the fuse that ignited their secession. After 70 years of struggling to maintain their sovereignty, the Southern States would now create anew the Republic of their fathers. Secession came swiftly on the heels of the presidential election of November 1860. One month later, South Carolina exercised her sovereignty, declaring herself free from the Constitutional compact of the union.

> *AN ORDINANCE to dissolve the union between the State of South Carolina and other States united with her under the compact entitled, "The Constitution of The United States of America."*
>
> *We the people of the State of South Carolina, in convention assembled, do declare and ordain, and it is hereby declared and ordained, That the ordinance adopted by us in convention on the twenty-third day of May, in the year of our Lord one thousand seven hundred and eighty-eight, whereby the Constitution of the United States of America was ratified, and also all acts and parts of acts of the General Assembly of this State, are hereby repealed; and that the union now subsisting between South Carolina and other States, under the name of the 'United States of America,' is hereby dissolved.*

Done at Charleston the twentieth day of December, in the year of our Lord one thousand eight hundred and sixty.[2]

Three weeks later, Mississippi followed South Carolina's lead, prompting Jefferson Davis to resign his seat as one of Mississippi's two United States Senators. In his resignation from the Senate, Davis eloquently defended the Constitutional right of secession.

I well remember an occasion when Massachusetts was arraigned before the bar of the Senate, and when the doctrine of coercion was rife, and to be applied against her, because of the rescue of a fugitive slave in Boston. My opinion then was the same that it is now. Not in a spirit of egotism, but to show that I am not influenced in my opinions because the case is my own, I refer to that time and that occasion as containing the opinion which I then entertained, and on which my present conduct is based. I then said that if Massachusetts—following her purpose through a stated line of conduct—chose to take the last step, which separates her from the Union, it is her right to go, and I will neither vote one dollar nor one man to coerce her back; but I will say to her, Godspeed, in memory of the kind associations which once existed between her and the other States.

It has been a conviction of pressing necessity—it has been a belief that we are to be deprived in the Union of the rights which our fathers bequeathed to us—which has brought Mississippi to her present decision. She has heard proclaimed the theory that all men are created free and equal, and this made the basis of an attack upon her social institutions; and the sacred Declaration of Independence has been invoked to maintain the position of the equality of the races. That Declaration is to be construed by the circumstances and purposes for which it was made. The communities were declaring their independence; the people of those communities were asserting that no man was born—to use the language of Mr. Jefferson—booted and spurred, to ride over the rest of mankind; that men were created equal—meaning the men of the political community; that there was no divine right to rule; that no man inherited the right to govern; that there were no classes by which power and place descended to families; but that all stations were equally within the grasp of each member of the body politic. These were the great principles they announced; these were the purposes for which they made their declaration; these were the ends to which their enunciation was directed. They have no reference to the slave; else, how happened it that among the items of arraignment against George III was that he endeavored to do just what the North has been endeavoring of late to do, to stir up insurrection among our slaves? Had the Declaration announced that the negroes were free and equal, how was the prince to be arraigned for raising up insurrection among them? And how was this to be enumerated among the high crimes which caused the colonies to sever their connection with the mother-country? When our Constitution was formed, the same idea was rendered more palpable; for there we find provision made for that very class of persons as property; they were not put upon the equality of footing with white men—not even upon that of paupers and convicts; but, so far as representation was concerned, were discriminated against as a lower caste, only to be represented in the numerical proportion of three-fifths. So stands the compact which binds us together.

Then, Senators, we recur to the principles upon which our Government was founded; and when you deny them, and when you deny us the right to withdraw from a Government which, thus perverted, threatens to be

> *destructive of our rights, we but tread in the path of our fathers when we proclaim our independence and take the hazard. This is done, not in hostility to others, not to injure any section of the country, not even for our own pecuniary benefit, but from the high and solemn motive of defending and protecting the rights we inherited, and which it is our duty to transmit unshorn to our children.[3]*

To the end of his life, Davis continued to defend State sovereignty. In his monumental work, *The Rise and Fall of The Confederate Government*, published in 1881, eight years before his death, he wrote,

> *The formation of a 'more perfect union' was accomplished by the organization of a government more complete in its various branches, legislative, executive, and judicial, and by the delegation to this Government of certain additional powers or functions which had previously been exercised by the Governments of the respective States—especially in providing the means of operating directly upon individuals for the enforcement of its legitimately delegated authority. There was no abandonment nor modification of the essential principle of a compact between sovereigns, which applied to the one case as fully as to the other. There was not the slightest intimation of so radical a revolution as the surrender of the sovereignty of the contracting parties would have been. The additional powers conferred upon the Federal Government by the Constitution were merely transfers of some of those possessed by the State governments—not subtractions from the reserved and inalienable sovereignty of the political communities which conferred them. It was merely the institution of a new agent who, however enlarged his powers might be, would still remain subordinate and responsible to the source from which they were derived—that of the*

sovereign people of each State. It was an amended Union, not a consolidation.

Entirely in accord with these truths are the arguments of Mr. Madison in the "Federalist," to show that the great principles of the Constitution are substantially the same as those of the Articles of Confederation. He says: "I ask, What are these principles? Do they require that, in the establishment of the Constitution, the States should be regarded as distinct and independent sovereigns? They are so regarded by the Constitution proposed. . . . Do these principles, in fine, require that the powers of the General Government should be limited, and that, beyond this limit, the States should be left in possession of their sovereignty and independence? We have seen that, in the new Government as in the old, the general powers are limited; and that the States, in all un-enumerated cases, are left in the enjoyment of their sovereign and independent jurisdiction.[4]

The establishment of the union under the Constitution abolished neither State sovereignty nor a State's right to leave the union into which it had voluntarily entered. Davis wrote, "It was not necessary in the Constitution to affirm the right of secession, because it was an attribute of sovereignty, and the States had reserved all which they had not delegated."[5] A common theme in the secession ordinances was the resumption of state powers previously delegated to the federal government. Arkansas' secession ordinance said, "The State of Arkansas hereby resumes to herself all rights and powers heretofore delegated to the United States of America."[6] North Carolina said the union between that State and others comprising the United States was dissolved and that, "the State of North Carolina is in full possession and exercise of all those rights of sovereignty which belong and appertain to a free and independent State."[7] After declaring its bonds with the union dissolved, Missouri said, ". . . and the State of Missouri, resuming the sovereignty granted by compact to the said United States upon admission of said State into the Federal Union, does again take its place as a free and independent republic amongst the nations of the earth."[8] Upon repealing its June 25, 1788, ratification of the Constitution, Virginia's Assembly decreed that "the State of Virginia is in full possession and exercise of all the rights of sovereignty which belong to a free and independent State."[9] Although it was expressed in various ways, State sovereignty was the common thread in all of the secession ordinances. Whatever the underlying causes of secession were, secession itself was based on States' rights and attempts by the seceding States to retain their sovereignty.

The only difference between the seceding States in 1860-61 and the seceding colonies in 1776 was that the colonies acted in concert while the seceding States acted individually. But at least two Southern States called for a new union. In its secession ordinance, Mississippi said, "That the people of the State of Mississippi hereby consent to form a federal union with such of the States as may have seceded or may secede from the Union of the United States of America, upon the basis of the present Constitution of the said United States, except such parts thereof as embrace other portions than such seceding States."[10] Alabama's secession ordinance went even further, setting the time and place for forming a new union and inviting specific states to join them in it:

". . . And as it is the purpose and desire of the People of Alabama to meet the slaveholding States of the South, who may approve such purpose, in order to frame a provisional as well as permanent Government upon the principles of the Constitution of the United States,

> *Be it resolved by the people of Alabama in Convention assembled, That the people of the States of Delaware, Maryland, Virginia, North Carolina, South Carolina,*

Florida, Georgia, Mississippi, Louisiana, Texas, Arkansas, Tennessee, Kentucky and Missouri, be and are hereby invited to meet the people of the State of Alabama, by their Delegates, in Convention, on the 4th day of February, A. D., 1861, at the city of Montgomery, in the State of Alabama, for the purpose of consulting with each other as the most effectual mode of securing concerted and harmonious action in whatever measures may be deemed most desirable for our common peace and security.

And be it further resolved, That the President of this Convention, be and is hereby instructed to transmit forthwith a copy of the foregoing Preamble, Ordinance, and Resolutions to the Governors of the several States named in said resolutions.[11]

South Carolina was the first to pass a secession ordinance on December 20, 1860, followed by Mississippi, January 9, 1861; Florida, January 10, 1861; Alabama, January 11, 1861; Georgia, January 19, 1861; Louisiana, January 26, 1861; and Texas, February 1, 1861. Other states passed secession ordinances later in the year. Notable examples were Virginia which seceded April 17, 1861 after Lincoln called for 75,000 volunteers to invade the Southern States, and Arkansas which passed its ordinance May 6, 1861 after federal troops occupied that State. Tennessee's was enacted May 6, 1861, North Carolina's on May 20, 1861, Missouri's on October 31, 1861, after federal troops imposed martial law in that State, and Kentucky's on November 20, 1861.

---

[1] Abraham Lincoln, First Inaugural Address, March 4, 1861.

[2] South Carolina Secession Ordinance, December 20, 1860.

³ Jefferson Davis, Farewell Speech to U. S. Senate, January, 1861.

⁴ Jefferson Davis, *Rise and Fall . . .*, vol. 1, , pp. 169-170.

⁵*Ibid.*, p. 169.

⁶ Arkansas Secession Ordinance, May 6, 1861.

⁷ North Carolina Secession Ordinance, May 20, 1861.

⁸ Missouri Secession Ordinance, October 31, 1861.

⁹ Virginia Secession Ordinance, April 17, 1861.

¹⁰ Mississippi Secession Ordinance, January 9, 1861.

¹¹ Alabama Secession Ordinance, January 11, 1861.

Chapter 9

A Republic of Sovereign States

LESS THAN A MONTH after Alabama invited other seceding States to create a new union, they met in Montgomery and formed a provisional government for the Confederate States of America. Jefferson Davis of Mississippi was elected Provisional President. In his inaugural address, Davis again defended the legality of secession as a right of State sovereignty:

Our present condition, achieved in a manner unprecedented in the history of nations, illustrates the American idea that governments rest upon the consent of the governed, and that it is the right of the people to alter or abolish governments whenever they become destructive of the ends for which they were established.

The declared purpose of the compact of union from which we have withdrawn, was 'to establish justice, insure domestic tranquility, provide for the common defense, promote the general welfare;' and when in the judgment of the sovereign States now composing this Confederacy, it had been perverted from the purposes for which it was ordained, and had ceased to answer the ends for which it was established, a peaceful appeal to the ballot-box, declared that so far as they were concerned, the government created by that compact should cease to exist. In this they merely asserted a right which the Declaration of Independence of 1776 had defined to be inalienable. Of the time and occasion for its exercise, they as sovereigns, were the final judges, each for itself. The impartial and enlightened verdict of mankind will vindicate the rectitude of our conduct, and He who knows the hearts of men will judge of the sincerity with which we laboured to preserve the government of our fathers in its spirit. The right solemnly proclaimed at the birth of the States and which has been affirmed and re-affirmed in the bills of rights of States subsequently admitted into the Union of 1789, undeniably recognizes in the people the power to resume the authority delegated for the purposes of government. Thus the sovereign States, here represented, proceeded to form this Confederacy, and it is by abuse of language that their act has been denominated a revolution. They formed a new alliance, but within each State its government has remained, and the rights of person and property have not been disturbed.[1]

Davis' First Inaugural address did not contain the saber-rattling rhetoric of Lincoln's March 4th speech. Lincoln threatened force against the seceding States, but Davis took a conciliatory position, saying, "There can, however, be but little rivalry between ours and any manufacturing or navigating community, such as the Northeastern States of the American Union," but adding that, "As a necessity, not a choice, we have resorted to the remedy of separation , and henceforth our energies must be directed to the conduct of our own affairs, and the perpetuity of the Confederacy which we have formed . . . But if this be denied to us, and the integrity of our territory and jurisdiction be assailed, it will but remain for us with firm resolve to appeal to arms and invoke the blessing of Providence on a just cause."[2] Lincoln's threat of force was an offensive one but Davis' reference to an "appeal to arms" was a defensive posture to maintain the newly declared freedom of the seceded States.

Lincoln maintained that "no State, upon its own mere motion, can lawfully get out of the Union—that resolves and ordinances to that effect are legally void, and that acts of violence, within any State or States, against the authority of the United States, are insurrectionary or revolutionary, according to circumstances." This was his declaration that the Southern States had not actually left the union, but remained in it as revolutionaries—a position he maintained throughout the War Between the States. His assertion that, ". . . acts of violence, within any State or States, against the authority of the United States, are insurrectionary and revolutionary," was empty rhetoric. Neither the seceding states individually, nor the Confederacy collectively, threatened violence against the North and none had declared war on the Union. The Confederacy sought only to go its own way and take its place among the nations of the world.

One week after Lincoln's first inaugural address, the Confederate Congress, comprised of members from the seven States of South Carolina, Mississippi, Georgia, Florida, Alabama, Louisiana and Texas, unanimously adopted a Constitution for the new country. Adopted March 11, 1861, the document embodied the intent of State Sovereignty in the United States Constitution of 1787. That was specifically included in its Preamble:

> *We, the people of the Confederate States, each State acting in its sovereign and independent character, in order to form a more permanent federal government, establish justice, insure domestic tranquillity, and secure the blessings of liberty to ourselves and our posterity—invoking the favour and guidance of Almighty God—do ordain and establish this Constitution for the Confederate States of America.*[3]

The Confederate Constitution's Preamble differs in two ways from that of the United States Constitution, and those two differences are significant. The first is the explicit affirmation of state sovereignty and the second is the invocation of God's "favor and guidance," which was absent from the Constitution of 1787. Other differences between the two documents are significant, reflecting the Confederate States' efforts to provide safeguards against over-weening national power that would destroy the rights of the States. One of those is the prohibition in the Confederate Constitution of federal funding for "internal improvements" unless those are paid for by the commercial interests whom they benefit. This would not allow one section of the country to receive benefits from the government at the expense of another, as had been the case in the union:

> *...neither this, nor any other clause contained in the Constitution, shall ever be construed to delegate the power to Congress to appropriate money for any internal improvement intended to facilitate commerce; except for the purpose of furnishing lights, beacons, and buoys, and other aid to navigation upon the coasts, and the improvement of harbours and the removing of obstructions in river navigation, in all which cases, such duties shall be laid on the navigation facilitated thereby, as may be necessary to pay the costs and expenses thereof.*[4]

The Confederate States also incorporated the Bill of Rights within the body of their Constitution, not as amendments that were attached to the United States Constitution after it was ratified.

In 1890, F. D. Srygley authored a book entitled, *Seventy Years in Dixie*, in which he chronicled Southern history from 1820 to 1890 through interviews with Southerners who had lived in that period. He recorded the testimony of one who was not a Southern planter, but a commoner of that period:

> ... *it seems queer to hear Southern men and women spoken of as 'traitors,' 'rebels,' 'enemies of American liberty' and 'foes of the Constitution'... nothing but patriotism pure and simple moved them to vote secession and to enlist in the army. The people at the South felt just as confident that the people at the North contemplated a deliberate overthrow of the Republic as their fathers in the Revolution felt that King George was a tyrant.... They understood that the Constitution of the United States was assailed, and that they were offering themselves for its defense. The question, as they understood it, was whether American liberty should be perpetuated or crushed by Northern monarchy.... in seceding the South held on to the Constitution, and the Declaration of Independence.... We traitors?... Did not everybody know that the North had set aside the Constitution, throttled our liberty and pulled the tail feathers out of the American eagle?* [5]

Written into the Confederate Constitution was also an anti-slavery provision that modern historians choose to either forget or ignore.

> *The importation of negroes of the African race from any foreign country other than the slaveholding States or Territories of the United States of America, is hereby forbidden; and the Congress is required to pass such laws as shall effectually prevent the same.*

> *Congress shall also have power to prohibit the introduction of slaves from any State not a member of, or Territory not belonging to, this Confederacy.* [6]

The federal compact into which the States had entered no longer protected their sovereign rights. Having voluntarily entered into that compact for such protection, some of those

States consequently exercised their sovereign right to leave it when it failed in its obligations to them. It was not the United States Constitution which failed, but the compact of States under it in which the Northern states sought supremacy over all others, and guarantees against a repetition of those failures were written into the Confederate Constitution. The South only desired to go its separate way, having no territorial aims on any other State or on the federal government in Washington. Jefferson Davis clearly expressed that to the world in April 1861:

> *We feel that our cause is just and holy; we protest solemnly in the face of mankind that we desire peace at any sacrifice save that of honour and independence; we ask no conquest, no aggrandisement, no concession of any kind from the States with which we were lately confederated; all we ask is to be let alone; that those who never held power over us shall not now attempt our subjugation by arms.*[7]

For decades, Southerners had witnessed the erosion of State sovereignty upon which the Republic was founded and through which they had ratified the United States Constitution. The steady encroachment of federal power, fueled by nationalistic aims of a Northern industrial/political complex, reached its zenith in the election of 1860. Federalist dreams of a consolidated, centralized power over the States were about to be realized, constituting a state of war against the sovereign States. The Whig-turned-Republican/Nationalist, Abraham Lincoln, would soon wield his Imperial axe in the final dismantling of State sovereignty. Constitutional government would be safe on the North American Continent for at least four more years in the South. That would not be the case in the North.

[1] Jefferson Davis, First Inaugural Address, February 18, 1861.

[2] *Ibid.*

[3] Preamble, Constitution of The Confederate States of America, March 11, 1861.

[4] Article I, Section 8, Constitution of The Confederate States of America.

[5] F. D. Srygley, *Seventy Years In Dixie* (The Gospel Advocate Co., Nashville: 1954), pp. 334- 335.

[6] Constitution of the Confederate States of America, Article 9, Sections 1 and 2.

[7] Jefferson Davis, Address to Confederate Congress, April 29, 1861.

Chapter 10

Lincoln's War on Northern Sovereignty

OBSESSED WITH SUBJUGATING the South, Lincoln not only made war upon the Confederacy, but upon his own people in the North. In a swift move to silence Northern critics of his war, he suspended Constitutional rights in the United States only a month after he was inaugurated.

The writ of habeas corpus was embodied in England's charter of freedom, the Magna Carta, and allowed for a prisoner of state to be released from prison by following established legal procedures. It is a most important ingredient of the rule of law in a free country that protects citizens from arbitrary arrest and imprisonment by the state for political reasons. American citizens accused of crimes have a constitutional right to a speedy public trial by an impartial jury, to be informed of the nature and cause of the accusation, to be confronted with witnesses against them, to bring witnesses in their favor, and to have the assistance of legal counsel. On April 27, 1861, Lincoln decided that such constitutional freedoms were no longer necessary and ordered the military to enforce his suspension of them. This suspension remained in effect for Lincoln's entire administration."[1]

"In May 1861 a special election was held to fill ten empty seats in the Maryland House of Delegates. The men elected were all leading industrialists, physicians, judges, and lawyers from Baltimore. But because they were suspected of harboring secessionist sympathies, most of them were arrested (without being charged) and sent to military prisons without trial, while a few of them fled."[2]

No one was exempt from Lincoln's anti-constitutional crusade to root out and punish all opposition to his scheme of empire—not even members of Congress, or the Judiciary. Responding to Lincoln's call for 75,000 militia troops to invade the South, the 6th Massachusetts Regiment marched through Baltimore on its way to change trains to Washington. Marylanders, who were sympathetic to the South, objected, and a riot broke out resulting in a number of troops and civilians killed. In the aftermath of the riot, both the Baltimore mayor and Maryland's governor declared that they would permit no more federal troops to pass through their state. Incensed by their announcements, Lincoln suspended the writ of habeas corpus in Maryland. Consequently, Lt. John Merryman, an officer in the Maryland militia, was arrested and imprisoned for allegedly impeding federal troop movements in Maryland. When he appealed for release on a writ of habeas corpus, his appeal was refused. In response, United States Chief Justice Roger Taney ruled that Lincoln's suspension of habeas corpus was illegal and that only Congress had such power. Lincoln ignored Taney's ruling and retaliated by ordering an arrest warrant to be issued for Taney. Lincoln later rescinded his order when a controversy arose over who would serve the warrant.

Lincoln's wrath was felt by other critics in high places. William M. Merrick, associate justice of the United States Circuit Court for the District of Columbia, was placed under house arrest in 1861 when he defied Lincoln's suspension of habeas corpus by issuing the writ. Another of Lincoln's targets was Ohio Congressman Clement L. Vallandigham, an anti-war Northern Democrat who criticized Lincoln's policies—especially his denial of Constitutional rights. General Ambrose Burnside, who was commander of the Ohio Military District, issued his infamous Order No. 38 in 1861 declaring that no toleration would be entertained for those expressing sympathy with the Confederacy. In a speech following Burnside's order, Vallandigham again criticized Lincoln's prosecution of the war against the South. Four days later the Congressman was arrested for violating Burnside's order, held without writ of habeas corpus, tried by a military tribunal, and deported to Canada. He was saved from imprisonment only by Lincoln's fear of making him a martyr.

So far as Lincoln was concerned, the Bill of Rights no longer existed. He not only interfered with State governments, orchestrated local elections and denied accused persons the writ of habeas corpus, he also targeted the press in violation of the First Amendment:

"Lincoln saw anyone who disagreed with him as a possible' traitor.' This included dozens of prominent newspaper editors and owners who, while in favor of the Union, were critical of Lincoln and his policies. That, of course, is why they were imprisoned. Lincoln's response to such dissent was to shut down dozens of newspapers and arrest and imprison their editors. On February 2, 1862, the Federal government began censoring all telegraph communication in the United States as well.

". . . In May 1861 the Journal of Commerce published a list of more than a hundred Northern newspapers that had editorialized against going to war. The Lincoln administration responded by ordering the Postmaster General to deny these papers mail delivery. At that time, nearly all newspaper deliveries were made by mail, so this action put every one of the papers out of circulation. Some of them resumed publication after promising not to criticize the Lincoln government."[3]

Lincoln's usurpation of unconstitutional powers during the War Between The States is unparalleled in American history. Not even John Adams, with his Alien and Sedition Acts, could compare with the absolute rule of Lincoln and his Republican Party over the Union from 1861 onward.

"The administration protected itself from criminal prosecution for depriving so many citizens of their constitutional rights by orchestrating the passage of an 'indemnity act' in 1863 that placed the president, his cabinet, and the military above the law with regard to unconstitutional and arbitrary arrests. This law was at odds with the centuries-old principle that no man (especially a government official) is above the law. . . . The indemnity law (sponsored by Pennsylvania Representative Thaddeus Stevens) never received enough votes from the U. S. Senate to become law; the presiding officer of the Senate simply declared the law valid, adjourned the Senate, and let the dissenters voice their protests."[4]

The abolition of Constitutional liberties in the North was starkly contrasted with the exercise of those same liberties in the South under the Confederate Constitution. Confederate President Jefferson Davis pointed that out in his Second Inaugural address:

> *For proof of the sincerity of our purpose to maintain our ancient institutions, we may point to the Constitution of the Confederacy and the laws enacted under it, as well as to the fact that through all the necessities of an unequal struggle there has been no act on our part to impair personal liberty or the freedom of speech, of thought or of the press. The courts have been open, the judicial functions duly executed, and every right of the peaceful citizen maintained as securely as if a war of invasion had not disturbed the land.*[5]

Lincoln's pretext for denying Constitutional liberties in the North was the war. He maintained that those liberties could be abrogated by the executive as a "war measure." Davis said no such action had been taken in the Confederacy, even "through all the necessities of an unequal struggle." Banished from the North because of war, Constitutional government still flourished in the Confederacy despite the same war.

As tyrannical as Lincoln was to his own people in the North, nothing compares with the absolute horror that he visited upon the sovereign State of Missouri between 1861 and 1865. Before Missouri's secession on October 31, 1861, martial law had been declared in the State by General John C. Fremont and would last throughout the four-year conflict. Led by such notables as William Quantrill and "Bloody Bill" Anderson, Missouri guerillas waged a four-year war against federal occupation troops. In one sense, "Reconstruction" came to Missouri four years earlier than the other Southern States.

"To be sure, several thousand Missourians lost their lives and property as a direct result of the war, but many more suffered the complete abrogation of their civil rights. At the present day, when there is apprehension in some circles concerning the weakening of civil law and individual rights and liberty, it is interesting to examine the conditions which existed when an entire state had all the protection afforded them by law and the Constitution stripped away for a period of nearly four years."[6]

Fremont had acted on his own initiative in imposing martial law in August 1861. General Halleck, who succeeded Fremont in command of Union troops in Missouri, found no written authorization for imposing martial law in the state. When Halleck inquired about the matter he was authorized by Lincoln to "suspend the writ of habeas corpus and to exercise martial law in his department where he deemed it necessary."[7] Interestingly, Lincoln's authorization came on November 1, 1861, the day following passage of Missouri's secession ordinance. Under the heel of martial law, the voluntary nature of the union created in 1787 was obliterated in Missouri. No longer was union loyalty in Missouri a matter of personal volition, but of coercion. "As early as April, 1862, Bernard G. Farrar, departmental provost marshal general, advised the district commanders that all men suspected of 'disloyalty' should be arrested and held in jail until they took oaths and put up bonds."[8] That prompted the issuance and posting of the following order by General Egbert Brown:

I. It is therefore ordered that all citizens within the limits of the southwestern division of the District of Missouri shall at once appear before some properly qualified officer and take the oath of allegiance to the United States of America and to the Provisional Government of the State of Missouri, and receive a certificate thereof, unless they have already done so.

II. Every citizen who fails to obey the above order will be deprived of the ordinary privileges of loyal citizenship. He shall neither hold any office nor be permitted to vote. He shall not be allowed to serve as a juror or appear as a witness . . . He shall not be permitted to pass at will on the public highway, but as punishment for the apparent aid and countenance which he extends to the marauders who are preying upon the country he is declared to be a prisoner within the limits of his own premises.[9]

While Lincoln was eliminating Constitutional rights in the North, he was prosecuting a military war against the Confederate States. His merciless "total war" on the South was a concurrent war on the Republic and every sacred principle upon which it was founded.

[1] DiLorenzo, *The Real Lincoln*, p. 135.

[2] *Ibid.*, pp. 138-139.

[3] *Ibid.*, p. 145.

[4] *Ibid.*, pp. 139, 140.

[5] Jefferson Davis, Second Inaugural Address, Richmond, Virginia, February 22, 1862.

[6] . Richard S. Brownlee, *Gray Ghosts of The Confederacy* (Louisiana State University Press: Baton Rouge, 1991), p. 142.

[7] *Ibid.*, p. 146.

[8] *Ibid.*, p. 158.

[9] *Official Records of the War of the Rebellion,* Series 1, vol. XIII, p. 435: General Order Fifteen, dated June 16, 1862, as cited in Brownlee, p. 158.

Chapter 11

Lincoln's War on Southern Sovereignty

CHARLESTON, SOUTH CAROLINA was a major port of entry in the South where the federal government collected import duties. At the mouth of Charleston Harbor stood Fort Sumter which was held by United States troops after South Carolina's secession. Fort Sumter was one of only two Southern military installations still in the hands of the United States in the South after secession. The other was Fort Barrancas, garrisoned under command of Lieutenant Adam Slemmer, in the harbor at Pensacola, Florida. Fort Pickens was a stronger facility in Pensacola harbor and after Florida seceded on January 9, 1861 State authorities made plans to take over Fort Pickens. Hearing rumors of its seizure, Lt. Slemmer moved his command from Fort Barrancas to Fort Pickens on January 10, 1861. That led Colonel William H. Chase, commander of Florida troops, to demand its surrender to the State of Florida. Slemmer refused but subsequent negotiations between Chase and Slemmer led to an armistice between the State of Florida and federal authorities in Washington.

The following timeline traces events that culminated in an armistice between the United States government and the State of Florida regarding the status of Fort Pickens during the final days of the Buchanan administration. (Armistice timeline adapted from *Lincoln Takes Command* by John S. Tilley.)

January 15, 1861 - Florida officers, Colonel Chase and Captain Ferrand, meet with Lieutenants Slemmer and Gilman pleading with them to avert bloodshed.

January 16, 1861 - Lieutenant Slemmer replies that he will hold Fort Pickens.

January 21, 1861 - General of the Army Winfield Scott secretly orders Captain Israel Vodges to embark his artillery company on the "USS Brooklyn" to reinforce Fort Pickens.

January 24, 1861 - Mail service from Pensacola is cut off to Fort Pickens and Slemmer writes Chase asking him to authorize resumption of mail service to the fort.

January 26, 1861 - Chase cordially replies to Slemmer and assures him mail service will be resumed. He also offers to supply Slemmer's command with provisions.

January 26, 1861 - A Montgomery newspaper reports the mission of the "USS Brooklyn."

January 28, 1861 - Senator Stephen R. Mallory of Florida warns President Buchanan that the "Brooklyn's" mission will mean war and asks for calm.

January 29, 1861 - U. S. Navy Captain Barron is sent on orders from the U. S. Navy Secretary to Florida to investigate. He reports relations are amicable and it would be wise to have the "Brooklyn" lay off outside the harbor. President Buchanan follows his recommendation.

January 29, 1861 - U. S. Secretaries of War and Navy reach an armistice accord with Colonel Chase and Florida authorities stipulating no attempt will be made to take Fort Pickens by Confederate forces if it is not reinforced and that no reinforcement will be made by U. S. authorities unless the Confederacy attacks the fort.

The armistice between the United States government and Florida authorities remained in force until after Lincoln was inaugurated March 4th. Calling it a "quasi armistice," Lincoln ignored its provisions and proceeded to reinforce Pickens, which was accomplished at midnight, April 12, 1861, when Vodges' troops were landed.

South Carolina seceded in December 1860, and Florida in January 1861. Lincoln would not become president until March 4, 1861 but he was already scheming to precipitate war with the South. In a brazen act before his inauguration, Lincoln sent a message to "E. B, Washburne for secret transmittal to General Winfield Scott."[1] The message said, "Please present my respects to the general, and tell him, confidentially, I shall be obliged to him to be as well prepared as he can to either hold or retake the forts, as the case may require, at or after the inauguration."[2]

The site where Fort Sumter was located was the property of the sovereign State of South Carolina. On March 24, 1794, the United States Congress passed an act providing for the erection of forts for the defense of certain ports and harbors in the United States. The sites of those forts were ceded by the States and were to be used solely for the purpose for which they were granted, but the ultimate ownership of the soil—or eminent domain— remained with the States in which they were situated.

By legislative enactment in 1805, South Carolina ceded to the United States in Charleston Harbor—and on the Beaufort River—various sites for the erection of forts. It has been claimed that these sites were purchased by the federal government. That is false. The Act of 1794 clearly stated that, "no purchase shall be made where such lands are the property of the State." Fort Sumter was the property of the sovereign State of South Carolina. But undeterred by Constitution or statute, Lincoln intended to have war and secretly dispatched troops to reinforce Fort Sumter. As early as February 1861, General Winfield Scott was secretly scheming with his subordinates to send an expedition to Fort Sumter to goad the South into firing the first shot.

While covert plans were underway in Tokyo for the Imperial Japanese Navy to strike the American fleet at Pearl Harbor in December 1941, Japanese government envoys were in Washington for "talks." It is conceivable that the Japanese took their strategy from Lincoln—only in reverse. During the time he was making secret plans to violate the armistice between the United States and Florida, Lincoln refused to see Confederate peace envoys sent to Washington but assured them through Secretary of State William H. Seward that the federal government had no designs on either of the forts. On March 29th, Lincoln "ordered three ships with 300 men and provisions to be ready to go to Fort Sumter."[3] On April 7th, Lincoln ordered the ships to Sumter and another to proceed to Fort Pickens while, on that same day, Seward was directed to inform the Confederate envoys, "that they had no design to reinforce Fort Sumter."[4]

At that very moment Lincoln's troops were steaming toward Charleston Harbor, ostensibly to "resupply" Fort Sumter, despite the fact that Major Anderson had South Carolina's permission to purchase supplies for his troops from the Charleston markets. Refusing to recognize the sovereign rights of the States, Lincoln vowed that the "Union is unbroken" and that, "the laws of the Union be faithfully executed in all the States." To Lincoln, "union" took precedence over anyone's liberty, and knowing they would not agree to the war he intended to begin, he consulted neither his cabinet nor Congress before ordering troops to Pickens and Sumter.

Lincoln got what he wanted in his gambit to "resupply" Fort Sumter. Confederate batteries opened up on the supply ship, then bombarded the fort while U.S. Navy warships stood offshore without firing a shot. Confederates were goaded into firing the first shot and Lincoln had his pretext for calling up State militias to invade the South. His call for 75,000 troops to put down what he called "the rebellion," was the straw that broke the camel's back and drove Virginia from the union. Lincoln's deceit and violation of the armistice was the first act of aggression in the war. The War Between The States was one of conquest, initiated by Lincoln and waged upon the South in violation of every sacred principle our founding documents express.

In the first two years of Lincoln's war on the South, the Union fared badly, due in large part to the military skill of Southern commanders who were greatly outnumbered and whose resources were no match for the Union. Among the best known of those commanders was Robert E. Lee. In April 1861, Lee was offered command of the United States Army, but refused after Lincoln's call for 75,000 volunteers to invade the South. Lee's allegiance was to his home and his state. In 1861, there was no such thing as a "citizen of the United States." Individuals were citizens of their sovereign States, and that was Lee's position when he turned down the offer and resigned his commission.

Arlington, Washington City P. O.
20 April, 1861

Lt Gen Winfield Scott
Comm of the Army

Gen

Since my interview with you on the 18 April, I have felt that I ought not longer retain my Commission in the Army. I therefore tender my resignation, which I request you will recommend for acceptance.

It would have been presented at once but for the struggle it has cost me to separate from a service to which I have directed all the best years of my life, and all the ability I possessed.

During the whole of that time, more than 30 years, I have experienced nothing but kindness from my Superiors, & the most cordial friendship from my companions. To no one Gen have I been as much indebted as to yourself for uniform kindness and consideration & it has always been my ardent desire to merit your affection.

I shall carry with me to the grave the most grateful recollections of your kind consideration & your name and fame will always be dear to me. Save in the defense of my native State, I never desire again to draw my sword.

Be pleased to accept my most earnest wishes for the continuance of your happiness, prosperity & believe me most truly yours.

R.E. Lee [5]

Lee did again draw his sword, but only—as he said—in defense of his native Virginia. Following the July 1861 Battle of First Manassas which sent federal troops in terrified flight back to Washington, the South was jubilant. Many thought that battle would decide the conflict and the South would be free. But Lincoln would have none of that. His oft-stated paramount aim was to "preserve the Union," and he would sacrifice every liberty and every last vestige of State sovereignty in the North and South to consolidate his union empire. In terms of human lives, he had launched the costliest war in America's history and before it ended more than 600,000 would die for him to realize his dream of American Empire.

In the war's first two years Confederate forces won a number of victories against great odds under brilliant commanders like Lee, Jackson, Stuart and Beauregard. Confederate success in the Peninsula Campaign from April to July 1862, was followed by Lee's march into Maryland in September where his Army of Northern Virginia met Union General George B. McClellan's Army of the Potomac at Sharpsburg. The Battle of Sharpsburg that began September 17, 1862, did not result in a clear-cut victory for either side, but it was considered a strategic Union victory. That was enough to give Lincoln an excuse to issue his unconstitutional gimcrack called, "The Emancipation Proclamation." Since slavery was protected by the Constitution emancipation could be legally accomplished only by a Constitutional amendment. But that was no barrier to Lincoln who erased a Constitutional provision with the stroke of his dictatorial pen.

Whereas on the twenty-second day of September, A.D. 1862, a proclamation was issued by the President of the United States, containing, among other things, the following, to wit:

That on the first day of January, A.D. 1863, all persons held as slaves within any state or designated part of a state, the people whereof shall then be in rebellion against the United States, shall be then, thenceforward, and forever free; and the executive government of the United States, including the military and naval authority thereof, will recognize and maintain the freedom of such persons and will do no act or acts to repress such persons or any of them, in any efforts they may make for their actual freedom.

That the executive will on the first day of January aforesaid, by proclamation, designate the states and parts of states, if any, in which the people thereof, respectively, shall then be in rebellion against the United States, and the fact that any state or the people thereof shall on that day be in good faith represented in the Congress of the United States by members chosen thereto at elections wherein a majority of the qualified voters of such states have participated shall, in the absence of strong countervailing testimony, be deemed conclusive evidence that such state and the people thereof are not then in rebellion against the United States.

Now, therefore, I, Abraham Lincoln, President of the United States, by virtue of the power in me vested as Commander-in-Chief of the Army and Navy of the United States in time of actual armed rebellion against the authority and government of the United States, and as a fit and necessary war measure for suppressing said rebellion, do, on this first day of January, 1863, and in accordance with my purpose to do so, publicly proclaimed for the full period of one hundred days from the first day above mentioned, order and designate as the states and parts of states, wherein the people thereof, respectively, are this day in rebellion against the United States the following, to wit:

Arkansas, Texas, Louisiana (except the parishes of St. Bernard, Plaquemines, Jefferson, St. John, St. Charles, St. James, Ascension, Assumption, Terrebonne, Lafourche, St. Mary, St. Martin, and Orleans, including the city of New Orleans), Mississippi, Alabama, Florida, Georgia, South Carolina, North Carolina, and Virginia (except the forty-eight counties designated as West Virginia, and also the counties of Berkeley, Accomac, Northampton, Elizabeth City, York, Princess Anne, and Norfolk, including the cities of Norfolk and Portsmouth), and which excepted parts are for the present left precisely as if this proclamation were not issued.

And by virtue of the power and for the purpose aforesaid, I do order and declare that all persons within said designated states and parts of states are, and henceforward shall be free; and that the executive government of the United States, including the military and naval authorities thereof, will recognize and maintain the freedom of said persons.

And I hereby enjoin upon the people so declared to be free to abstain from all violence, unless in necessary self-defense; and I recommend to them that, in all cases when allowed, they labor faithfully for reasonable wages. And I further declare and make known that such persons of suitable condition will be received into the armed services of the United States to garrison forts, positions, stations, and other places, and to man vessels of all sorts in said service.

And upon this act, Sincerely believed to be an act of justice, warranted by the constitution upon military necessity, I invoke the considerate judgment of mankind and the gracious favor of Almighty God.[6]

As a legal document, the Emancipation Proclamation was worthless and violated both the letter and spirit of the Constitution. It struck down the Constitutional provision allowing slavery without legally amending the Constitution and repealed the Fugitive Slave Law without Congressional action. Consider the following points:

1. If Lincoln commenced his war to free slaves, why did he wait a year and a half after its commencement to issue his proclamation? And why did he then delay its implementation for another 100 days?

2. Lincoln's proclamation freed no slaves in the United States. It exempted all Southern territory then under Union control and actually freed no slaves in the South because the South was not under United States jurisdiction. Of course, Lincoln did not recognize secession and regarded the Confederacy as "in rebellion" and still under federal authority.

3. The rationale that this proclamation was made under his authority as a "fit and necessary war measure," is patently dictatorial. Slavery was protected under the Constitution of 1787 and that could only be changed by amending the Constitution. No president has authority to negate a part of the Constitution as Lincoln did with a stroke of his pen.

4. According to Lincoln, a state of war automatically abolishes Constitutional rights. That is evident in claiming this act was, "warranted by the constitution as a military necessity." By what stretch of the imagination could the abolition of slavery be construed as a "war measure?" His "military necessity" was simply a public relations ploy to prevent Britain from intervening on the side of the South,

5. His charge to "freed" persons to work for "reasonable wages" is laughable. Where would they obtain employment for wages? Slaves in the South were not freed by his proclamation and he exempted slaves in U. S. controlled areas from its provisions. Every person who was a slave on December 31, 1862 was still a slave on January 1, 1863. Lincoln was counting on slaves fleeing to the Union army to provide cannon fodder for his war machine.

After Chancellorsville, Confederate fortunes worsened as Lincoln and his generals plotted "total war" against the South. The plan was to not only engage the Confederacy's military forces in battle, but to ravage, pillage and destroy everything in the Union Army's path, including homes, crops, and livestock. The atrocities committed against Southern civilians throughout the war would bring courts martial today and brand the perpetrators as war criminals. Why Lincoln and his military henchmen have never been arraigned and condemned before history's bar of justice for their war crimes is unexplainable.

From the war's onset, Northern religionists and their abolitionist allies viewed it as a struggle of their righteousness against the "evil" South and that they—like their Puritan fathers—were God's instrument for meting out His wrath. That was the thesis of Northern preaching and of Julia Ward Howe's "Battle Hymn of The Republic."

"Mrs. Howe was not a Bible-believing Christian. She was a Unitarian Transcendentalist. As a Unitarian, her religious views were not based on fundamental theocentric doctrines of the Scriptures, but upon the anthropocentric beliefs of the higher critics of her day. . . . By her own statements, it is very clear as to what her opinion was concerning Jesus Christ. She was quoted in her biography saying, 'Not until the Civil War [*sic*] did I officially join the Unitarian church and accept the fact that Christ was merely a great teacher with no higher claim to preeminence in wisdom, goodness, and power than any other man.'

"In her Battle Hymn, Mrs. Howe arrogantly applied the apocalyptic judgment of *Revelation* (14:17-20 & 19:15) to the Confederate Nation. She pictured the Union army not only as that instrument which would cause Southern blood to flow out upon the earth, but also as the very expression of God's word.

"...from the moment these lines were first sung, when the Union Army first crossed onto Southern soil, the troops, via the strains of this song, were (according to Howe) authorized agents of the Lord's work. Thenceforth, of the nearly 700,000 lives lost in that internecine war, the Union dead fell as martyrs, with a special place awaiting them in heaven. But Confederate soldiers or even Southern non-combatants were Satan's minions, the plebian others, deserving of death and no hereafter.

"Simply stated, this Battle Hymn was used as war propaganda to legitimize a cause for the Northern soldiers and citizens in their bloody invasion and destruction of the South."[7]

As the Puritans regarded their imposition of civil and religious rule in Ireland as the work of God, so the North viewed itself as God's instrument to destroy the South.

"Among the ranks of Northern patriotic clergy, none perceived the sacred dimensions of America more clearly than Horace Bushnell. From his opening salvo in 1861 on 'Reverses Needed,' Bushnell revealed that he perceived in bloodshed something mystically religious and moral that was creating a nation where only inchoate states and loose confederations had previously existed. . . . Neither slavery nor the 'North' nor the 'South' defined the war for Bushnell so much as the fruition of a providential Christian state, conceived by the Puritans, rearticulated in the Declaration of Independence, and actualized through civil war [sic] . . . By late 1863 this war that was not self-consciously fought for the creation of an American civil religion was unintentionally becoming about the creation of an American civil religion that would grow as the killing endured."[8]

The theocracy envisioned by the Puritans and advocated by Northern religionists like Bushnell had no place for State sovereignty. Their secular theocracy was the equivalent of Hitler's, "Ein Volk, Ein Reich, Ein Fuhrer," and that was the nation Lincoln envisioned. The only thing that stood in his way was the stubborn resistance of the South which was fighting for North America's last remnants of Constitutional liberty and

State sovereignty. With the help of his political cronies and Northern clergymen, all of that was about to change.

"Rarely, if ever, has a major denomination endorsed one party over another since the Civil War [sic]. But in 1864, when passions ran high, 'the whole moral influence' of the church had become captive of the state and its Republican orthodoxy. Lincoln's wager paid handsome dividends as participants redefined the 'cause' of war to mean emancipation, thereby justifying not only total war for unconditional surrender but also Republican hegemony."9

"By 1864 the pulpit had become, in effect, a political platform for Republican rule. Clearly, nothing short of devastation would do. The enabling words 'God' and 'Providence' no longer needed to be invoked. 'Manhood,' 'patriotism,' and 'common sense' could do it all, and they required 'strangulation.'"10

In the end, the "strangulation" of the South would be completed when Lincoln unleashed his blue-coated Huns upon Southern civilians. Union General William T. Sherman will forever live in infamy in the hearts of Southerners. The English language has no words to describe his utter wickedness. If ever a human being became totally depraved and devoid of all goodness, it was Sherman. "Sherman's religion was America, and America's God was a jealous God of law and order, such that all who resisted were reprobates who deserved death. . . . Thus absolved of all responsibilities of accountability, Sherman could blame the enemy for anything and everything that happened to them. They deserved it."11

With Lincoln's blessing, Sherman marched across Georgia, accountable to no law higher than his own fiat and without shame or moral restraint. Jesus said, "Not that which goeth into the mouth defileth a man; but that which cometh out of the mouth, this defileth a man. . . . For out of the heart proceed evil thoughts, murders, adulteries, fornications, thefts, false witness, blasphemies."¹² Good and evil originate in the heart and a man's true nature is determined by the words proceeding from his heart. Recorded in government documents from Lincoln's war, Sherman's words express the evil in his vile soul: "The Government of the United States has . . . any and all rights which they choose to enforce in war—to take their lives, their homes, their lands, their everything . . . War is simply power unrestrained by constitution."¹³

Sherman, who later turned his venom upon the Plains Indians, massacring women, children, the old and the infirm, wrote to Lincoln's Secretary of War Edwin M. Stanton that, "There is a class of people [Southerners] men, women, and children, who must be killed or banished before you can hope for peace and order."¹⁴ The total destruction of the Southern people with their means of production and livelihood was Lincoln's goal, which he would accomplish through Sherman. The Southern States—once and for all—would do obeisance to the government of Hamilton, Clay and Lincoln.

Sherman was merciless in his path of destruction across Georgia and South Carolina. He destroyed homes, crops, and animals, killed many civilians, and left total devastation in his wake.

"As Sherman explained in a famous letter to his adjutant R. M. Sawyer, the enemy was subject to the government and its armies such that 'any and all rights which [the generals] choose to enforce the war—to take their lives, their homes, their lands, their everything—was permissible. . . . And almost alone among Civil War [*sic*] generals, Sherman forsook God as well as the rules of war, and, to all appearances, never entertained the possibility that Providence would make him pay."¹⁵

With Lincoln's approval of his war on civilians, Sherman swept across Georgia unfettered by any moral consideration. Jefferson Davis Tant, who later became a gospel preacher in Texas, described his family's extreme hardships at the hands of Sherman's vandals.

> *I was born in Paulding County, Georgia, 1861. I was only eight days old when my father started for the war, and was four years old when he returned. I was taught that he was my father and that I must respect him. When father started to the war, we owned eleven farms in North Georgia, and we were considered 'well-to-do.' Our home was on the New Hope Church battleground. After the battle nothing was left on the farm but some oak trees. My dear mother and oldest brother walked 22 miles to where they heard of a wheat field outside of the army's march, and pulled up two bushels of wheat, beat it out on a rail the next day, and brought it home. For three months we lived under an oak tree, with nothing to eat except boiled wheat with salted water put in it. The salt was obtained by my mother's digging up the ground where the smokehouse had stood and boiling the dirt to get the salt from it. . . . We were in the line of Sherman's march through Georgia, 60 miles wide and 300 miles long. Not a cow, horse, hog, nor house was left. All were burned or taken. Germany in her bloodiest days was never any meaner than the Yankee soldiers under Sherman.[16]*

Identical pogroms were perpetrated in the Valley of Virginia under Union commanders Philip Sheridan, David Hunter, and George A. Custer. The following eyewitness account from the son of Virginia's ex-Governor John Letcher described the devastation of Lexington and the burning of the Letcher house.

> *The officers and men sent by Hunter to do the work at once surrounded the house and plundered it—while the others of them were pouring something flammable over the furniture and setting fire to it. They refused to allow*

my mother to have anything carried out, not even a change of clothes; everything was destroyed that was not stolen. One officer, whose name we never knew, offered to assist in saving valuables: he got a trunk, but Captain Berry of a Pennsylvania Regiment who was in charge of the burning, refused to let him carry it out: an altercation followed when a soldier picked up the trunk and carried it into the yard. Captain Berry ordered other things that some persons were attempting to carry out to be seized and thrown into the burning building. All the buildings were burned. The roof of my grandmother's house caught fire and when a Negro servant tried to extinguish it, the soldiers threatened to shoot him if he did not come down. . . . Captain Berry and many of his soldiers were extremely rude and insulting to my mother and sister. No reason, except the order of General Hunter, was given for burning our house. Washington College was plundered, apparatus destroyed, books torn up, etc.[17]

North Carolina suffered the same Yankee atrocities. When Confederate forces burned the town of Plymouth, North Carolina during combat, Major General J. G. Foster of the Union Army wrote a letter to Confederate Major General D. H. Hill chastising him for that action. In his reply to Foster's letter, Hill blistered him for the atrocities committed by Yankee forces against Southern civilians in that State.

Goldsborough, North Carolina, March 24, 1863
Major General J. G. FOSTER, Federal Army.

SIR:

Two communications have been referred to me as the successor of General French. The prisoners from Swindell's company and the Seventh North Carolina are true prisoners of war and if not paroled I will retaliate five-fold.

In regard to your first communication touching the burning of Plymouth you seem to have forgotten two things. You forget, sir, that you are a Yankee and that Plymouth is a Southern town. It is no business of yours if we choose to burn one of our own towns. A meddling Yankee troubles himself about every body's matters except his own and repents of everybody's sins except his own. We are a different people. Should the Yankees burn a Union village in Connecticut or a cod-fish town in Massachusetts we would not meddle with them but rather bid them God-speed in their work of purifying the atmosphere.

Your second act of forgetfulness consists in your not remembering that you are the most atrocious house-burner as yet unhung in the wide universe. Let me remind you of the fact that you have made two raids when you were weary of debauching in your negro harem and when you knew that your forces outnumbered the Confederates five to one.

Your whole line of march has been marked by burning churches, school-houses, private residences, barns, stables, gin-houses, negro cabins, fences in the row, &c. Your men have plundered the country of all that it contained and wantonly destroyed what they could not carry off. Before you started on your freebooting expedition toward Tarborough you addressed your soldiers in the town of Washington and told them that you were going to take them to a rich country full of plunder. With such a hint to your thieves it is not wonderful that your raid was characterized by rapine, pillage, arson and murder. Learning last December that there was but a single weak brigade on this line you tore yourself from the arms of sable beauty and moved out with 15,000 men on a grand marauding foray.

You partially burned Kinston and entirely destroyed the village of White Hall. The elegant mansion of the planter and the hut of the poor farmer and fisherman were alike consumed by your brigands. How matchless is the impudence which in view of this wholesale arson can complain of the burning of Plymouth in the heat of action! But there is another species of effrontery which New England itself cannot excel. When you return to your harem from one of these Union-restoring excursions you write to your Government the deliberate lie that you have discovered a large and increasing Union sentiment in this State. No one knows better than yourself that there is not a respectable man in North Carolina in any condition of life who is not utterly and irrevocably opposed to union with your hated and hateful people. A few wealthy men have meanly and falsely professed Union sentiments to save their property and a few ignorant fishermen have joined your ranks but to betray you when the opportunity offers. No one knows better than yourself that our people are true as steel and that our poorer classes have excelled the wealthy in their devotion to our cause.

You knowingly and willfully lie when you speak of a Union sentiment in this brave, noble and patriotic State. Wherever the trained and disciplined soldiers of North Carolina have met the Federal forces you have been scattered as leaves before the hurricane.

In conclusion let me inform you that I will receive no more white flags from you except the one which covers your surrender of the scene of your lust, your debauchery and your crimes. No one dislikes New England more cordially than I do, but there are thousands of honorable men even there who abhor your career fully as much as I do.

Sincerely and truly, your enemy,

*D. H. HILL,
Major-General, C. S. Army* [18]

When Sherman burned Atlanta, "Lincoln was far less concerned with Sherman's conduct of the war (which he approved) than the implications of the Atlanta victory for the upcoming national election."[19] Lincoln was nearing his dream of federal hegemony over the States and his "total war" would make that dream a reality. The Constitutional right of the individual's security of life and property meant nothing to Lincoln. His apologists argue that "this was war," but Lincoln never recognized the right of secession. So far as he was concerned, the South and her people were still in the Union and he made that clear in his first Inaugural Address when he said the union was "perpetual" and "the Union is unbroken." If he really believed that, then Southern civilians had their rights to life and property protected by the U. S. Constitution. The atrocities he authorized against them is prima facie evidence of his total disregard for the Constitution and forever brands him a despot of the deepest dye.

With overwhelming superiority in manpower, weapons, and manufacturing resources, Lincoln's army in Georgia, South Carolina and Virginia stripped the land like a plague of locusts. With Lee's Army of Northern Virginia starving, the war of attrition against the South came to an end at Appomattox, April 9, 1865. Lincoln's war had cost 618,000 American soldiers' lives, a death toll that exceeded the combined number of Americans subsequently killed in World War One, World War Two and Vietnam. On a single day in Lincoln's war, 23,582 Americans were killed at the Battle of Sharpsburg. That single day's death toll was more than the combined total of Americans killed in the Revolutionary War, the War of 1812, the Spanish American War and the Mexican War. Lincoln went to his grave with the blood of more than a half million of his countrymen on his hands, but not before he had destroyed Constitutional government and State sovereignty.

Few persons realized that, or suffered its consequences, more than former Confederate President Jefferson Davis. When its military surrendered, the Confederate government fled southward. Davis was captured by federal troops in Georgia on May 10, 1865. A week later he was incarcerated in leg irons at Fort Monroe, Virginia, and placed under 24-hour guard with a lamp burning in his cell day and night. General Halleck, Fort Monroe's commander, objected to placing Davis in manacles, but Assistant Secretary of War, C. A. Dana directed General Nelson Miles to shackle Davis, which he did the day after Davis arrived at Fort Monroe. Davis' ill treatment at the hands of the military brought a public outcry and the manacles were removed, but his long imprisonment without trial had only begun.

In June 1865, Davis was indicted by a federal court in Virginia on the charge of "Directing armed rebellion against the United States." Another indictment on the same charge was brought against him in the District of Columbia later that year, but he never faced any of those charges in court. Davis fervently hoped he would have his day in court to legally vindicate the right secession, but Lincoln's heirs deprived him of that opportunity.

The government determined that Davis' trial would have to be in a civil court in Virginia, but Virginia's federal circuit judge, John Underwood, said he had no jurisdiction in the matter because Virginia was under martial law and Davis was being held by military authorities. U. S. Supreme Court Chief Justice

Salmon P. Chase agreed, allowing both magistrates to refuse Davis a writ of habeas corpus—more of Lincoln's legacy. Davis languished in Fort Monroe for two years without trial, until his release on a $100,000 bond was secured May 13, 1867 by—of all people—Horace Greeley editor and publisher of the *New York Tribune*, along with some other Northerners and ten Richmond business men. Greeley had editorialized about Davis' ill treatment at Fort Monroe, calling it, "one of the worst tortures known to humanity."

It appeared to many people that Chase was being lenient by refusing to bring Davis to trial. That was not so. He had good reason for refusing to arraign Davis before the bar of justice, even after his associate, Circuit Judge John C. Underwood for the district of Virginia, bragged to a Congressional committee in 1866 that he could pack a jury to insure Davis' conviction. Chase knew such a trial would navigate dangerous legal waters, and told President Andrew Johnson, "Do not let Davis take the stand. He will vindicate the right of Southern secession." So, finally, after years of exhausting his excuses, Chase argued that ratification of the 14th amendment to the Constitution in 1868 would constitute "double jeopardy" for Davis if he was brought to trial for treason. On February 15, 1869, when the case was docketed for trial, the government indicated it would not prosecute Davis. The government knew its case could not stand the scrutiny of truth in a court of justice.

Chase's twisting of the Constitution mirrored Lincoln's perversion of it. His argument against trying Davis was based on the constitutional right against double jeopardy as stated in the Bill of Rights, but his conclusion was based on an unconstitutional amendment. The 14th Amendment is an ex post facto law, which violates Article 1, Section 9 of the Constitution. The term ex post facto refers to laws made under which a person is tried for action he took before the law made his action a crime. This amendment criminalized an oath of office to the Confederacy, which was not a crime on the books before 1868. Therefore, Davis would not have been put in "double jeopardy" by a trial because his actions prior to the adoption of the 14th Amendment were not criminal. By refusing to put Davis on trial, the federal government tacitly vindicated the right of secession

---

[1] Nicolay and Hay, *Lincoln*, III, 250, as cited in John Shipley Tilley, *Lincoln Takes Command* (Nippert Publishing, Ashland City, TN: 1991), p. 106.

[2] *Ibid.*

[3] *Ibid.*

[4] *Ibid.*

[5] Robert E. Lee, Letter of Resignation From United States Army, April 20, 1861.

[6] Emancipation Proclamation, *Living American Documents*, Star, Todd, Curtis, eds. (Harcourt, Brace & World, Inc., NY: 1961), pp. 184 - 185.

[7] R. Michael Givens, "It Is Our Duty," *Confederate Veteran*, vol. 67, No. 5 (September/October 2009).

[8] Harry S. Stout, *Upon the Altar of The Nation*, (Penguin Books: 2006), p. 249.

[9] *Ibid.*, p. 389.

[10] *Ibid.*, p. 385.

[11] *Ibid.*, p. 371.

[12] *Holy Bible*, Matthew 15: 11, 19.

[13] William T. Sherman, January 31, 1864, *Official Records, vol. XXX*II, p. 280.

[14] *Ibid.*, vol. XXXIX, p. 132.

[15] Stout, pp. 400- 401.

[16] Fanning Yater Tant, *J. D. Tant, Texas Preacher* (Faith and Facts Press, Indianapolis: 1958), pp. 19-20.

[17] Henry Kyd Douglas, *I Rode With Stonewall* (Fawcett Publications, Greenwich Conn.: 1961), p. 277.

[18] *Official Records*, Series 2, vo. 5 (Prisoners of War), pp. 389-390.

[19] Stout, p. 372.

Chapter 12

"The Final Solution"

THREE DAYS AFTER LEE surrendered at Appomattox John Wilkes Booth assassinated Abraham Lincoln at Ford's Theater in Washington. Lincoln's death was tragic; not that he was dead, for he deserved to die. The tragedy was that he escaped the hangman's noose for his war crimes. Instead, his assassination apotheosized a criminal and deified him in the minds of historical revisionists. With a single shot, Booth rendered Lincoln a national god to be exalted, adored, quoted, and emulated forever after.

"Besides seeking vengeance Northern preachers, writers, and statesmen immediately set out to complete Lincoln's incarnation as the messiah of the reunited Republic. . . . George Boardman explained to his Presbyterian congregation in Binghamton, New York, that the only parallel to Lincoln was Christ: 'His murderer has effected his apotheosis. Our beloved chief magistrate was removed at the height of his fame, his reputation unsullied, the equal of Washington, and beyond Washington, a martyr to the cause of Constitutional liberty. The name of ABRAHAM LINCOLN has entered into history, almost the only one without a spot."[1]

That a man who orchestrated the destruction of civilian life and property—it is estimated that at least 50,000 Southern civilians died at the hands of Union troops—could be compared with the sinless Son of God is utterly blasphemous. And it is doubtful that deported Ohio Congressman Vallindigham or Northern editors who were imprisoned for criticizing Lincoln's war would call him "a martyr to Constitutional liberty." But with his canonization by Booth's bullet, frenzied, vengeance-seeking Northerners wallowed in Lincoln-worship and would continue to treat the South in peace as he had in war.

From that time until the present, conventional wisdom has claimed Lincoln would have been magnanimous to the South following the war. His record of barbarities against Southerners during the war belies that notion. The fact remains that the task of "reconstruction" fell to his successor, Andrew Johnson, and Lincoln's Republican Party. It is postulated that Johnson's policies toward the prostrate South tended toward a measure of sovereignty for their States and were extensions of Lincoln's. That is probably not the case. Although Johnson was a Unionist, he was a Southerner, and his policies were probably affected by that fact. One cannot definitively say what Lincoln would have done after the war. That he would have welcomed the South back with open arms is a contrivance of the Lincoln cult. What one can say is that Lincoln's party and policies were bequeathed to his followers and they acted toward the conquered South after the war in the same way that Lincoln did during the war.

"Reconstruction"—a misnomer—is another of those words bandied about by politically correct historians, evoking images of Southern recovery like the U. S. sponsored recovery in Europe and Japan following World War Two. Germany and Japan were rebuilt under the aegis of the United States and both have reclaimed their places in the world of nations. Their recovery was facilitated by the infusion of billions of federal dollars into their economies. Compare that with the punishment inflicted upon the South and the theft of Southern money by Northern Republicans in the guise of "Reconstruction." The first phase of reconstruction was begun under Lincoln's successor, Andrew Johnson. His plan called for amnesty for Southerners who would sign an oath of allegiance. "Exceptions to the offer . . . included important Confederate officials and Confederates who owned more than $20,000 worth of property. This seemed to exclude the leaders of the Old South."[2] After the oath was signed, voters in the Southern States were to call constitutional conventions, "repeal the state's ordinance of secession, abolish slavery, and repudiate Confederate government and state debts. Then the State would be allowed to elect a new government and send representatives to Washington."[3] These terms that Southerners thought would be the sum of reconstruction were met by all of them by the end of 1865. But Northern politicians had other plans.

Military victory wasn't enough. "Vengeance" became the cry in the North. Former Methodist circuit rider, William G. (Parson) Brownlow was governor of Tennessee from 1865 to 1869 and a vengeful Unionist who called for another war upon the South.

> *I am one who believes the war has ended too soon. We have whipped the rebels, but not enough. . . . The second army of invasion will, as they ought to, make the entire South as God found the earth, without form and void. They will not, and ought not to, leave one rebel fence-rail, outhouse, one dwelling, in the eleven seceded states. As for the rebel population, let them be exterminated. When the second war is wound up, which should be done with swift destruction, let the land be surveyed and sold out to pay expenses.*[4]

Another gubernatorial puppet of the Northern government was Andrew Jackson Hamilton, governor of Texas for 14 months following the war. An appointee of President Johnson, Hamilton also spoke at the Philadelphia Postwar Convention, calling for another war against the South. Further military action against the prostrate South never materialized, but not for lack of desire on the part of many Northerners. Instead, the Republican

Congress declared another kind of war on the South with passage of the Reconstruction Act of 1867. That measure ejected the Southern States from the Union, imposed military rule on them, and treated them as conquered provinces. Congressional Reconstruction was the second war against the South.

"The Reconstruction Act of 1867 declared that the Southern states were not part of the Union. Remember, this was the Union from which the North had previously said that these states could not withdraw! From 1866 to March 2, 1867, the Southern states were accorded the rights of statehood. They participated in the ratification of the Thirteenth Amendment and in the rejection of the Fourteenth Amendment. The rejection of the Fourteenth Amendment posed a major roadblock to the revolutionary schemes of the radicals in Congress. They knew that even after their successful military conquest of the Southern people, they could not complete their evil designs as long as the South retained even this slight amount of political power. To further their evil schemes the radicals decided to eject their conquered foe from Congress and then complete their revolution. To further their revolutionary and evil goals, the Northern element treated the Southern states alternately as states and as conquered territories."[5]

President Johnson's veto of the Reconstruction Act was quickly overridden by the Republican Congress and military rule was imposed upon the Southern States for the next 10 years. All of that was because the Southern States rejected the 14th Amendment. That amendment made a United States citizen of "All persons born and naturalized in the United States, and subject to the jurisdiction thereof." This effectively abolished primary citizenship in the states, further eroding State sovereignty. Henceforth, United States citizenship would take precedence over State citizenship. The amendment's second section prohibits any test for voting except "for participation in rebellion, or other crime." That deprived States from setting their own voter qualifications and gave that power to the federal government. Johnson's plan prohibited only former Confederate government officials from voting. The Congressional plan denied the vote to all Confederate soldiers and officers. By specifying that males 21 years of age were ineligible because of "participation in rebellion," the Republican Congress disenfranchised most white voters in the South. The third section prohibited any former U. S. official who had served the Confederacy from serving in Congress, being a presidential elector, or holding any civil or military office in State or federal government. Section four rejected any responsibility of the United States government to accept claims for debts incurred by Southern states for the war, including claims for emancipation of slaves. In the fourth section, the federal government gave itself power to take the property of anyone without due process of law, which violated the Constitution they were amending, and struck another massive blow in dismantling the Republic.

The significance of this illegal amendment cannot be overstated. Its rejection—especially by Southern States—resulted in the Reconstruction Act of 1867 that placed the conquered States of the South under military rule and occupation. The 14th Amendment was illegally adopted and should not be a part of the Constitution today.

"At the time of the introduction of the Fourteenth Amendment, there were thirty-seven states in the Union. By mid-1867, the federal Secretary of State had received official documents from the legislatures of thirty-three of the thirty-seven states giving the states' answer to the proposed Fourteenth Amendment. The result was a rejection of the radical amendment."[6]

The Kennedy brothers indicate that out of 37 States in the union, 28 were needed to ratify the 14th Amendment. Of the 37 states, 22 voted yes, 12 voted no, and three did not vote.

Mississippi's resolution rejecting the amendment did not reach Washington, and was counted among those who did not vote, but "even if the three non-voting states are added to the states voting for ratification, the amendment would still be short of the number needed for ratification."[7] Undaunted by failure, the Republican Congress ejected the Southern States from the Union and declared them conquered provinces. But even then, the 14th Amendment failed to be ratified when New Jersey, Ohio, and Oregon rescinded their ratifications and it remains today an illegal appendage to the U. S. Constitution.

"The First Reconstruction Act, passed in March 1867, divided the South into five military districts, wiping out its existing state governments. Under military supervision, each State was to elect a constitutional convention."[8] Under this arrangement, a flood of Northern opportunists known as "Carpetbaggers"—so-called because they brought their belongings with them in carpet bags—went South to make their fortunes off the misery of the Southern people. Carpetbaggers were installed in local government positions by Union military commanders where they could drain whatever meager resources the Southern people still possessed.

They were also instrumental in creating racial hatred between former slaves and Southern whites. This tactic—one still used by 21st century race-baiters—was designed to maintain their lucrative positions. The NAACP, Al Sharpton and Jesse Jackson need racial strife to stay in business today. Without it, money would cease to flow into their treasuries. In order to keep the money coming in, they must manufacture racial issues like the phony charge of a black woman's rape by white members of Duke University's Lacrosse team in 2006. The following first-hand account describes the same kind of race-baiting operations by carpetbaggers in East Texas during reconstruction.

The negroes did not know what to do with their newly acquired freedom and meddlers and mischief makers from the North, known as carpetbaggers, came down to put them on the right path and to show them how to keep it. The carpetbaggers told them that they were full fledged American citizens and in every way the equals of the proudest white people and that it was up to them to assert their rights. In other words, they made the negroes believe that the white people of the South were their worst enemies and that it was legitimate to wage any kind of warfare against such enemies. The police of the reconstruction governor, E. J. Davis, not only upheld and protected the negroes in their deviltry, but even instigated them to greater activity in that direction.

The white people countered by organizing what was known as the Ku Klux Klan. Knowing that the negroes were being used as mere tools by the carpetbaggers to annoy and trouble the South, the Ku Klux Klan did not wish to deal any more harshly with them than was necessary. They accordingly sought at first to quell them by playing upon their well known superstition. They adopted white robes and hoods. This mask appeared sufficiently ghostly, especially by moonlight, and it actually did frighten many a marauding negro back to his cabin and made him jolly well satisfied to stay there. But the hardier ones, backed by the carpetbaggers, rose above their superstition and began to commit greater outrages still.

Then the Ku Klux Klan began to shoot. There is no telling how many negroes the carpetbaggers caused to be killed. One morning I saw the bodies of five bullet-riddled negroes in a pile in Canton. On another occasion when I was on my way to Grand Saline, I saw the head of a white man at the top of a pole. The head had belonged to a carpetbagger who had the night before made an incendiary speech to a secret meeting of negroes in an abandoned ginhouse in a lonely region. The Ku Klux eavesdropped him, and caught him up when he was leaving the place of meeting. The trouble with the negroes extended over a period of about ten years, until the people put an end to carpetbag rule by electing the Hon. Richard Coke, regular Democratic nominee, Governor, and thereby putting an end to the rule of Governor Davis.[9]

With their sovereignty destroyed and deprived of a voice in their local and state governments, Southerners suffered the loss of their remaining resources to Northern Republican politicians who came South to collect the spoils. With white Southern voters disenfranchised and their governments under military rule, carpetbagger politicians had a free hand in plundering the former Confederate States. After describing the removal of Alabama Governor R. M. Patton by Major General George Meade, commander of the military district of which Alabama was a part, John S. Tilley wrote,

A glance at other members of the official family of Alabama will uncover the enormity of the political crime involved in bodily taking over a state's affairs and subjecting them to the whims of incompetent and unscrupulous Northern carpet-baggers. Prominent in the new administration were Bingham of New York, as state treasurer; Reynolds of Wisconsin, auditor; Miller of Maine, former agent of the Freedman's Bureau, secretary of state; Keffer of Pennsylvania, head of department of industrial relations; Morse, a scalawag, who was to use his new office to secure his own relief from a pending indictment for murder.[10]

Intent only on self-aggrandizement, Carpetbaggers were political leeches on the backs of Southern taxpayers. They occupied all local, state and federal government offices, leaving

Southerners without representation in their States or in Congress. Tilley says Alabama's Congressmen in 1868 were from Massachusetts, New York, Maine, Wisconsin, and Scotland, and its Senators were, "Spencer, indifferently of Iowa, Nebraska, Massachusetts, and Ohio, a wandering adventurer...[and] Warner, another non-resident..."[11] The *Montgomery Advertiser* reported the adjournment of the Alabama Legislature in 1869, saying, the carpetbaggers "have probably gone to Ohio, Maine, Massachusetts, Michigan, or wherever their families may be residing."[12]

Ignorance of Congressional district boundaries was no hindrance to carpetbagger politicians in Alabama. Selma, Alabama's newspaper reported that a man named, "Buckley, of Illinois, in conducting his campaign, was so ignorant of the political divisions of the state as to spend his money and waste his energies soliciting support in a county entirely outside his own district."[13]

Republican vengeance against Southerners extended to the very clothes they wore. Under reconstruction, the wearing of Confederate uniforms was forbidden under penalty of law. With their property destroyed and their land in ruins, many former soldiers returned home to find nothing left to them but the clothes they were wearing—their uniforms. Even those were banned. "The North prefers to disguise its crimes by referring to this period as 'Reconstruction.' In reality, it was a cruel, scandalous, and criminal oppression of an erstwhile free people!"[14]

> *None but those who went through this period have any conception of it. Defeat on the battlefield brought no dishonor, but all manner of oppressions. With poverty and enforced domination of a race lately in slavery, brought humiliation and required a courage little less than superhuman . . . After the surrender the soldiers*

returned to their homes where homes remained. They literally had nothing left but the ground upon which they stood. Families scattered, negroes freed, banks closed, no currency available, the slaveholder knowing less than his overseer and slaves about the practical part of farming. The lawyer had no clients, the teacher had no pupils, the merchant had no credit, the doctor had no drugs. O! It was pitiful.

The reconstruction period was not only a time of real oppression, but also a time of repression, suppression and fearful humiliation. The South lost more than $2 billion by loss of slaves, together with confiscated and destroyed property. The South was also left with a bonded war debt of $3 million.[15]

Added to the personal humiliations heaped upon Southerners during that dark period was the looting of public and private funds by Carpetbaggers. When the war ended, large amounts of cotton were stored in Southern warehouses. The crops produced during the war were prevented from export by the naval blockade of Southern ports so the cotton had been stored. After the war, U. S. "Treasury Agents" descended on the South to "seize for the Federal treasury the confiscated holdings of the Confederate government.[16] Issuing bonds in exchange for necessities during the war, the Confederate government, "in this way, had come into possession, or into the right of possession, of large amounts of cotton."[17] This put the Treasury Agents into the cotton business. They indiscriminately confiscated cotton from private owners, regardless of whether it fell under the Confederate bonds. The lucrative aspect of confiscating private property for the Federal treasury was that the "agents" received a percentage of the proceeds, "ranging from one-fourth to one-half of the property seized."[18] The tribute paid to the Federal government by the South was every bit as onerous as that exacted from the Jews by Publicans who served Rome. In 1865 it was revealed that, "in Alabama alone, 125,000 bales valued at some $37.5 million" was stolen, and "a cotton agent in Demopolis, Alabama, quite a young man, received for one month's services 400 bales of cotton, worth at the time at least $80,000.[19]

Reconstruction governments in the South were filled with politicians who sold their votes and enriched themselves on the backs of Southern taxpayers. The expenses for South Carolina's legislative session in 1872 amounted to about a million dollars, or approximately $11,000 per day, including salaries of $39,000 for 475 "clerks."[20] The story was the same in all the other former Confederate States. Northern politicians plundered, pillaged and prostrated the South into economic ruin. In South Carolina the tax collected for the State convention in 1868 was six times greater than the tax collected for the entire State in 1860. Southerners lost farms to the tax collectors that had been in their families for generations and tens of thousands of acres were sold at auction, stolen by carpetbaggers at pennies on the dollar. It's a pretty good guess how railroad tycoons like the Vanderbilts of New York were able to purchase a contiguous 125,000 acre estate in North Carolina on which they built the Biltmore House. Designed to further oppress the South, tariff laws were enacted making it cheaper to ship goods by rail from the North to the South than to ship goods from South to North, and those laws remained on the books until the 1950s.

Military occupation of the South ended in 1877, but reconstruction continued into the 20th century. The dismantling of the Republic was nearly completed and had Lincoln survived the assassin's bullet, he would have been pleased with his efforts. State sovereignty was a thing of the past. Lincoln's "national" vision had become a reality. That "government of the people, by the people, and for the people" had perished from the earth. What remained was a monolithic federal government in Washington that viewed all states as provinces subject to its dictates. Lincoln's words at Gettysburg were poetic but void of intellectual substance. Of that speech, H. L. Mencken wrote,

> . . .*But let us not forget that it is poetry, not logic; beauty, not sense. Think of the argument in it. Put into the cold words of everyday, the doctrine is simply this: that the Union soldiers who died at Gettysburg sacrificed their lives to the cause of self-determination—that government of the people, by the people, for the people, should not perish from the earth. It is difficult to imagine anything more untrue. The Union soldiers in the battle actually fought against self-determination; it was the Confederates who fought for the right of their people to govern themselves.*[21]

Lincoln said the Union soldiers at Gettysburg, "gave their lives that that nation might live," as though a Confederate victory would have marked the end of the United States. The Northern government would have continued as before—except with fewer states. The Confederacy would not have destroyed the Washington government, and had no desire to do so, but a century of Northern propaganda taught in public schools continues to promote that myth.

> *When the war ceased, the pretext on which it had been waged could no longer be alleged. The emancipation proclamation of Mr. Lincoln, which, when it was issued, he humorously admitted to be a nullity, had acquired validity by the action of the highest authority known to our institutions—the people assembled in their several State Conventions. The soldiers of the Confederacy had laid down their arms, had in good faith pledged themselves to abstain from further hostile operations, and had peacefully dispersed to their homes; there could not, then, have been further dread of them by the Government of the United States. The plea of necessity could, therefore, no longer exist for hostile demonstration against the people and States of the deceased Confederacy. Did vengeance, which stops at*

the grave, subside? Did real peace and the restoration of the States to their former rights and positions follow, as was promised on the restoration of the Union? Let the recital of the invasion of the reserved powers of the States, or the people, and the perversion of the republican form of government guaranteed to each State by the Constitution, answer the question. For the deplorable fact of the war, for the cruel manner in which it was waged, for the sad physical and yet sadder moral results it produced, the reader of these pages, I hope, will admit that the South, in the forum of conscience, stands fully acquitted.[22]

Confederate Major General Patrick Cleburne of Helena, Arkansas, was a commander in the Army of Tennessee. So devoted was he to State sovereignty that he once said, "If this cause that is so dear to my heart is doomed to fail, I pray heaven may let me fall with it, while my face is toward the enemy and my arm is battling for that which I know to be right." His prayer was answered when he fell in battle November 30, 1864, at Franklin, Tennessee. Eleven months before his death, Cleburne voiced his thoughts about the struggle for State sovereignty and the dire consequences that would ensue should it fail:

Every man should endeavor to understand the meaning of subjugation before it is too late. . . . It means the history of this heroic struggle will be written by the enemy; that our youth will be trained by Northern school teachers; will learn from Northern school books their version of the war; will be impressed by the influences of history and education to regard our gallant dead as traitors, and our maimed veterans as fit objects for derision. . . . It is said slavery is all we are fighting for, and if we give it up we give up all. Even if this were true, which we deny, slavery is not all our enemies are fighting for. It is merely the pretense to establish sectional superiority and a more centralized government, and to deprive us of our rights and liberties. [23]

General Cleburne was not a prophet, but a man of clear vision concerning Northern aims and what he predicted would happen with the fall of the Confederacy has come to pass.

---

[1] Stout, p. 449.

[2] Sellers and May, p. 217.

[3] *Ibid.*

[4] William G. ("Parson") Brownlow, Speech in Postwar Convention, Philadelphia, 1866.

[5] James Ronald Kennedy & Walter Donald Kennedy, *The South Was Right!* (Pelican Publishing, Gretna, LA: 1994), p. 168.

[6] *Ibid.,* p. 171.

[7] *Ibid.,* p. 172.

[8] Sellers and May, p. 219.

[9] Clyde Ellis, who was related to the author, and whose family migrated from Fayette County, Alabama, to Van Zandt County, Texas, in 1870, "Comments in Reference to The Ellis Family, as Recorded by My Father, A. S. Ellis." Obtained from Terry Thedford, Ben Wheeler, Texas.

[10] William H. Brantley, "Chief Justice Stone of Alabama" in Hilary A. Herbert, *Why the Solid South?,* as cited by John S. Tilley, p. 162

[11] *Ibid.,* p. 220; Walter L. Fleming, *Civil War and Reconstruction in Alabama,* pp.736-738, as cited by John S. Tilley, *The Coming of the Glory,* p. 163.

[12] *Montgomery Advertiser,* January 2, 1869, as cited by Tilley, p. 169.

[13] *The Southern Argus,* Selma, Alabama, June 30, 1869, as cited by Tilley, p. 166.

[14] *The South Was Right!,* p. 238.

[15] Mildred Lewis Rutherford, "Reconstruction Days, 1865-1876," *Confederate Veteran,* vol. XXXII, No. 8 (August, 1924), p. 306.

[16] Tilley, p 128.

[17] *Ibid.*

[18] Tilley, p 128.

[18] *Ibid.*

[19] *Ibid.,* p. 129- 130.

[20] *Ibid.,* p. 230.

[21] H. L. Mencken, *Smart Set Magazine,* May, 1920.

[22] Davis, Preface to *The Rise and Fall* . . . .

[23] Major General Patrick Cleburne, January 1864.

Chapter 13

Eliminating Sovereignty's Remnants

ALTHOUGH STATE SOVEREIGNTY was eliminated in the South, scattered remnants of it had to be removed from all other States in the decades after 1877. That was facilitated by continuing Republican majorities in Congress and Republican presidents who followed in Lincoln's steps. Following Lincoln's successor, Andrew Johnson, came Ulysses S. Grant, whose administration was filled with corruption and bribery, Rutherford B. Hayes, James A. Garfield, and Chester A. Arthur. Democrats did not win the presidency again until 20 years after Lincoln's death when Northern Democrat Grover Cleveland was elected in 1884. The latter decades of the 19th century and those of the early 20th century were devoted to consolidating the empire envisioned by Hamilton and Clay and established by Lincoln. Those decades witnessed the construction of federally subsidized transcontinental railroads, the near extermination of the Plains Indians to acquire their lands, the acquisition of overseas territory, and federal subsidies for Northern industrial barons.

In 1866, Robert E. Lee carried on a correspondence with British Lord John Dalberg Acton. Lord Acton, who had been sympathetic to the Southern cause, wrote Lee to request his views on the current state of American politics following the war.

Lord Acton was to furnish information from Lee to a British weekly Review and wrote to Lee,

If, Sir, you will consent to entertain my request, and will inform me of the light in which you would wish the current politics of America to be understood, I can pledge myself that the new Review shall follow the course which you prescribe...

Without presuming to describe the purely legal question, on which it seems evident to me from Madison's and Hamilton's papers that the Fathers of the Constitution were not agreed, I saw in State Rights the only availing check upon the absolutism of the sovereign will, and secession filled me with hope, not as the destruction but as the redemption of Democracy. The institutions of your Republic have not exercised on the old world the salutary and liberating influence which ought to have belonged to them, by reason of those defects and abuses of principle which the Confederate Constitution was expressly and wisely calculated to remedy. I believed that the example of that great Reform would have blessed all the races of mankind by establishing true freedom purged of the native dangers of Republics. Therefore I deemed that you were fighting the battles of our liberty, our progress, and our civilization; and I mourn for the stake which was lost at Richmond more deeply than I rejoice over that which was saved at Waterloo.[1]

In his reply to Lord Acton on December 15, 1866, Lee expressed his fear of a consolidated government that was, even then, being planned by Northern Republicans.

I can only say that while I have considered the preservation of the constitutional power of the General Government to be the foundation of our peace and safety at home and abroad, I yet believe that the

maintenance of the rights and authority reserved to the States and the people, not only essential to the adjustment and balance of the general system, but the safeguard to the continuance of a free government. I consider it the chief source of stability to our political system, whereas the consolidation of these States into one vast republic, sure to be aggressive abroad and despotic at home, will be the certain precursor of that ruin which has overwhelmed all those that have preceded it. I need not refer one so well acquainted as you are with American history, to the State papers of Washington and Jefferson, the representatives of the federal and democratic parties, denouncing consolidation and centralization of power, as tending to the subversion of State Governments and despotism. The New England states, whose citizens are the fiercest opponents of the Southern states, did not always avow the opinions they now advocate. Upon the purchase of Louisiana by Mr. Jefferson, they virtually asserted the right of secession through their prominent men; and in the convention which assembled at Hartford in 1814, they threatened the disruption of the Union unless the war should be discontinued. The assertion of this right has been repeatedly made by their politicians when their party was weak, and Massachusetts, the leading state in hostility to the South, declares in the preamble to her constitution, that the people of that commonwealth "have the sole and exclusive right of governing themselves as a free sovereign and independent state, and do, and forever hereafter shall, exercise and enjoy every power, jurisdiction, and right which is not, or may hereafter be by them expressly delegated to the United States of America in congress assembled." Such has been in substance the language of other State governments, and such the doctrine advocated by the leading men of the country for the last seventy years.[2]

One who is conversant with the past can more accurately gauge the future. Lee was an educated man who knew human nature and human governments and keenly understood the dangers of unbridled national power. As Lee predicted, the federal government became "aggressive abroad" by pursuing imperial aims in the war with Spain in 1898, by which it acquired vast colonial holdings in Cuba, Puerto Rico, and the Philippines. It later entered a European war in 1917 and today American youth are dying in Middle Eastern countries to impose an American-style "democracy" on them that they do not want. There is no difference in waging war to conquer the world and waging war to "spread democracy to the world." Both are self-serving.

Through the last decades of the 19th century, federal propaganda continued to chant the mantra of consolidated government. In his Inaugural Address on March 4, 1881—20 years to the day from Lincoln's first Inaugural—James A. Garfield echoed Lincoln's notion that the union was "perpetual," asserting its "supremacy" over the States.

> *The supremacy of the nation and its laws should be no longer a subject of debate. That discussion, which for half a century threatened the existence of the Union, was closed at last in the high court of war by a decree from which there is no appeal—that the Constitution and the laws made in pursuance thereof are and shall continue to be the supreme law of the land, binding alike upon the States and the people. This decree does not disturb the autonomy of the States nor interfere with their necessary rights of local self-government, but it does fix and establish the permanent supremacy of the Union.[3]*

His boast that, "the supremacy of the nation" was beyond debate was the Republicans' way of telling Southern States their sovereignty was gone. Perhaps he did not intend to do so, but Garfield admitted the North waged a war of conquest when he said the Constitution was binding upon the States by force of arms, "from which there is no appeal." He ignored the fact that the Constitution bound the federal government and limited its powers. The Constitution was designed to protect the sovereignty of the States from federal tyranny—not the other way around. In an exercise of semantic gymnastics, Garfield said, "this decree (the war) does not disturb the autonomy of the States . . . but it does fix and establish the permanent supremacy of the Union." There is a difference between "autonomy" and "sovereignty." A State's "autonomy" means it is self-governing, but a State may be self-governing without sovereignty. "Autonomy" and "sovereignty" are not synonymous. *The Britannic World Language Edition* of Funk & Wagnall's Standard Dictionary defines "autonomy" as "The condition or quality of being autonomous; especially the power or right of self-government." Of the word "sovereign," it says, "Free, independent and in no way limited by external authority or influence: a sovereign state" An autonomous State may govern itself but be limited by a higher authority. A sovereign State's power is limited by no authority higher than the will of its sovereign people. Modern States are autonomous, but they are not sovereign. Lincoln could not have said it better. The Union is permanently supreme as a result of his war and absolute power over the States finally rests in the hands of the federal government. Ironically, Garfield, who parroted the Lincoln/Webster creed of "perpetual union," met the same fate as Lincoln at the hands of an assassin.

Hitler ist Deutschland, Deutschland ist Hitler!

It isn't enough to conquer a people and exact tribute from them. The vanquished must be reprogrammed and pacified to accept their new order of government. Hitler did that by capturing the minds of Germany's youth and that was the ideal of late 19th century socialist and Baptist Minister, Francis

Bellamy. Francis' cousin, Edward Bellamy, was also a socialist who authored utopian novels in the late 1800s which captured the imagination of the rising socialist movement of that time.

Francis Bellamy was the author of the "Pledge of Allegiance." His avowed purpose in writing the pledge was to cement the idea of "one nation"—envisioned by Lincoln and Webster—in the minds of Americans, emphasizing its "indivisibility." His Pledge is a creedal affirmation of Lincoln's war to unite the American empire under one absolute government. By this Pledge, American minds have been conditioned to accept the new order of government that the Bellamys hoped would result in a socialist state—a hope which may be on the verge of realization in the United States.

"Francis Bellamy (1853-1931) . . . wrote the original Pledge in August 1892 . . . In his Pledge, he is expressing the ideas of his first cousin, Edward Bellamy, author of the American socialist utopian novels *Looking Backward* (1888) and *Equality* (1897).

"Francis Bellamy in his sermons and lectures and Edward Bellamy in his novels and articles described in detail how the middle class could create a planned economy with political, social and economic equality for all. The government would run a peace time economy similar to our present military industrial complex.

"In 1892 Francis Bellamy was also a chairman of a committee of state superintendents of education in the National Education Association. As its chairman, he prepared the program for the public schools' quadricentennial celebration for Columbus Day in 1892. He structured this public school program around a flag raising ceremony and a flag salute—his 'Pledge of Allegiance.'"[4]

Francis Bellamy was employed by *Youth's Companion* magazine which sold American flags to schools and as part of that effort, Bellamy became involved with the National Education Association. His Pledge was published in the September 8, 1892 issue of *Youth's Companion* and made its debut in public schools on Columbus Day that year. It originally read, "I pledge allegiance to my Flag and the Republic for which it stands, one nation indivisible, with liberty and justice for all." The word "to" was later added to read ". . . to the Republic. . ." The magazine also prescribed the salute to be given while saying the pledge. It mandated the gesture of an outstretched arm with the palm of the hand facing downward—identical to the Italian Fascists' salute of the 1920s which was later adopted by Hitler's Nazis. Those who have seen Nazi film maker Leni Riefensthal's "Triumph of The Will" may recall the images of uniform rows of massed humanity, standing as a solid phalanx, with outstretched arms, and vowing allegiance to the State personified in their Fuhrer. That was Bellamy's aim. School children today who stand and recite the Pledge of Allegiance each morning pledge themselves to a powerful centralized government that destroyed State sovereignty. More than a century of pledging allegiance to Lincoln's government and its "indivisible" lie has helped to pacify and brainwash a once sovereign people and laid the groundwork for further federal intrusion into every aspect of our lives.

Direct Taxes on Incomes

Former President Gerald Ford said, "A government big enough to give you everything you want is a government big enough to take from you everything you have." With the growth and power of Lincoln's government, a concurrent cry arose for government to be the patron of its citizens. Americans learned they could vote themselves largesse from the nation's purse and politicians found they could retain power by doling out government welfare money which, of course, necessitated more federal tax revenue. Unfettered by State sovereignty, a centralized federal government now easily enriches itself by confiscating its citizens' earnings.

Direct federal taxation began with the first income tax assessed against workers during Lincoln's first administration. Under the Revenue Act of 1861 all persons with incomes above $800 per year were taxed at three percent and those living outside the country were taxed at five percent. That was changed in 1862 when Lincoln signed another Revenue Act which progressively taxed incomes above $600 at three percent and those above $10,000 and persons living outside the United States at five percent. A third measure passed in 1864 created tax brackets. All three of those acts violated Article I, Section 9 of the Constitution, and Lincoln set the precedent for direct federal income taxes we pay today.

During the Constitutional Convention's debates, James Madison argued against the power of the federal government to levy direct taxes on the people of the states, saying, "the General Government will have powers far beyond those exercised by the British Parliament, when the States were part of the British Empire. It will in particular have the power, without the consent of the State Legislatures, to levy money directly on the people themselves." That is what Lincoln did in the 1860s and what was done 48 years after his war ended. The 16th Amendment, passed by Congress July 2, 1909, and ratified February 3, 1913, says, "The Congress shall have power to lay and collect taxes on incomes, from whatever source derived, without apportionment among the several States, and without regard to any census or enumeration." That amendment repealed the portion of Article I, Section 9 of the Constitution which said, "No capitation or other direct, Tax shall be laid unless in proportion to the Census or enumeration hereinbefore directed to be taken." Prior to the 16th Amendment, the federal government could only levy taxes in proportion to the population of a State, which protected the smaller States from a larger burden, and that was Madison's point. State sovereignty was further eroded and another remnant of the Republic was removed when the 16th Amendment was ratified and a direct federal income tax became permanent law in the 20th century.

Disarmament and Occupation

To maintain its power, an empire must see that its citizens are disarmed and its troops distributed throughout its domain in sufficient strength to respond immediately to any dissent. To accomplish that, the United States government stripped the sovereign states of control of their militias and deployed federal troops in every state.

The first militias were the citizens of the colonies—those "Minutemen" farmers who confronted the British at Concord—and that was the general organization of the military in the early days of the Republic. The federal government maintained only a small standing army. Each State provided its own militia which could be requested for federal service in time of national emergency. That arrangement was in effect in 1861 when Lincoln called on the States to furnish 75,000 volunteers to invade the South. Each militia was under the control of its respective state government and each State provided its troops to the federal government upon request of the president.

There was no such thing as a large standing United States Army at the beginning of the Republic. National defense was provided by state militias who supplemented the Republic's small army. That was the substance of the First Militia Act passed May 2, 1792, during Washington's administration. That measure authorized the president to call state militias into federal service upon invasion, or when federal law was opposed to such an extent that local judicial authorities could not handle the opposition. Six days later, on May 8th, Congress passed the Second Militia Act. That law organized militias according to the directives of the State Legislatures and conscripted all free white male persons between the ages of 18 and 45 for service. It also called for militia members to provide their own arms, bayonets and ammunition. The 1792 Militia Acts were later amended by the Militia Act of 1862 which permitted Negroes to serve in United States militias—a measure to provide cannon fodder for the North in its war against the South.

After 1865, that was no longer the case. The South could not be permitted to raise militias. It was Southern militias who answered the call when the South was invaded and if the military occupation of that region was to be effective those states could not have militias. Federal troops occupied the South during Reconstruction, quelling any tendency to raise State troops. But that wasn't enough. Washington had to control all of the troops in all of the states in order to further consolidate its power. After the War Between The States, the federal government maintained larger army units—especially cavalry units—to rid the plains of Indians and push its empire further westward.

The idea of a large standing army in the Republic was repugnant to the Founders and two of the earliest presidents addressed that in speeches. Of the principles he brought to the presidency, James Madison said one of those was, "to keep within the requisite limits a standing military force, always remembering that an armed and trained militia is the firmest bulwark of republics—that without standing armies their liberty can never be in danger, nor with large ones safe."[5] Andrew Jackson expressed the same sentiment. "Considering standing armies as dangerous to free governments in time of peace, I shall not seek to enlarge our present establishment"[6]

At the dawn of the 20th century, Congress passed yet another military measure—the Militia Act of 1903. This established the

National Guard as the primary reserve component for the U. S. military and placed the National Guard of each State under the control of the federal government. The National Guard was required to conform to the organization of the Federal Army and inspections of Guard units were to be conducted by Federal Army officers. In 1906, another national legislative act was passed to arm the National Guard. Federal funding meant federal control of the militias and effectively ended States' control of their armed forces. By this means, the federal government disarmed the States and took control of all armed forces within them. Each State now has a National Guard, but that organization is under federal control. State governors can call out their National Guard units in times of emergencies such as floods, destructive storms, or riots, but the States do not fully fund or control the Guard. If the federal government wants to call a State's National Guard for service overseas, as it has done many times and is now doing in the Middle East, the State has no power to prevent it from doing so. That is far different from Massachusetts' refusal to send its militia to fight the British in the War of 1812. The Militia Act of 1906 removed one of the final remnants of State sovereignty. It also provided for military occupation of every State by the national government through National Guard units, making once sovereign States into federal provinces that are disarmed—without militias—and occupied by United States troops. That occupation is further supplemented by Regular Army, Air Force and Naval installations in almost every State of the union.

Every State is now occupied by federal troops, but total disarmament of the people has not yet been accomplished. The right to keep and bear arms is one of the last rights Americans still possess, and perhaps the last bulwark against full blown tyranny in America. In recent years, numerous local jurisdictions have passed anti-gun laws to restrict gun ownership and eradicating the Second Amendment is high on the federal agenda. The "new birth of freedom" that Lincoln extolled at Gettysburg was, in reality, a "new birth of tyranny."

Chapter 14

In the Valley of Decision

THE SOUTH FOUGHT a devastating war on its own soil from 1861 to 1865 to preserve the Republic founded by the Constitution of 1787. Despite the just cause for which it fought, the South could not halt Lincoln's overwhelming Northern resources that destroyed the Republic. Southern men who knew what liberty was were willing to sacrifice their last full measure of devotion for it. Worthy of highest esteem, they laid their all on liberty's altar. They fought and they died, and with them died the Republic. Every State in the Union is today reaping the result of Lincoln's war on State sovereignty and the South's loss.

Taking money directly from State citizens by confiscatory taxation, the federal government doles portions of it back to those States with rules attached. In 2009, the Oklahoma Legislature authorized a state ballot question to amend its Constitution, making English the official language of Oklahoma. That action brought a letter from the United States Department of Justice to Oklahoma Attorney General Drew Edmondson on April 14, 2009, threatening the loss of federal funds for Oklahoma if the question passed:

"Many state, county and local jurisdictions receive, either directly or indirectly, federal assistance from the Department of Justice (DOJ) or other federal agencies. As you know, recipients of federal financial assistance must comply with various civil rights statutes including Title VI of the Civil Rights Act of 1964 . . . which prohibits discrimination on the basis of race, color, national origin. Under DOJ regulations implementing Title VI, recipients of federal financial assistance have a responsibility to ensure meaningful access to their programs and activities by LEP [limited English proficient] persons."[7]

When Oklahoma's Congressional delegation requested clarification of the letter, the DOJ backed down and said, "Please be assured that voter approval next year of Oklahoma's official English amendment would not affect the state's eligibility for financial assistance from the Department."[8] This not-so-veiled threat to cut off federal funds from Oklahoma is a prime example of blatant federal usurpation of State sovereignty. Following the letter clarifying the DOJ's position, Oklahoma's United States Senator, James Inhofe, said, "The threat to withhold funding by the Justice Department is further evidence of a runaway federal government improperly attempting to constrain state action."[9] Oklahoma's First District Congressman, John Sullivan, said, "As a firm believer in states' rights for Oklahoma, it is important that the people of Oklahoma are free to make this choice without threats from their own federal government."[10] Inhofe and Sullivan were the only two members of Oklahoma's Congressional delegation to touch the basic issue top, side or bottom. The others expressed satisfaction that Oklahoma would not lose federal funds. Sullivan and Inhofe defined the real issue—State's rights. State laws are routinely struck down by judicial fiat from the U. S. Supreme Court, but the Federal Department of Justice surpassed that by threatening action against Oklahoma before it passed a law and while that law was still being debated. Can anyone fathom such a letter being sent to a State by the administration of Thomas Jefferson?

There isn't a scintilla of Constitutional authority for the mandates handed down to the States by the federal bureaucracy, but most States meekly accept their provincial status as governors and legislators jostle each other for a place in the federal soup line. Docile, self-serving State politicians are elated to receive a cup of soup ladled from the pot that the federal government previously confiscated from their citizens. The only soup the federal government has is what it takes from State citizens who make it. Government is no longer about preserving the rights of the people. Modern government is about perpetuating federal power through "entitlements" doled out at taxpayer expense. Patrick Henry asked, "Is life so dear, or peace so sweet, as to be purchased at the price of chains and slavery?" The tragedy of our time is that many Americans, willing to trade liberty for a federal handout, resoundingly reply, "yes." Benjamin Franklin said, "They who would give up an essential liberty for temporary security, deserve neither liberty nor security." Lincoln "saved the union" by destroying the Republic and American liberties have been replaced with temporary security. The national government is now a "Nanny" to every strata of American society and the federal soup kitchen becomes more crowded with each passing generation.

The Constitutionality of granting federal money to individuals was debated in the U. S. Congress in 1828 when the widow of a deceased war veteran, who was a Major General, asked Congress for money equivalent to a year's pay for him. This was occasioned by his death after he had suffered financial loss and her request was essentially for a charitable contribution from the public treasury. Edward S. Ellis referred to this event during Davy Crockett's service as a United States Congressman from Tennessee in his 1884 work entitled, *The Life of Colonel David Crockett.* Ellis' account of Crockett's speech during debate on the request has been questioned, but it demonstrates how far afield the federal government has gone in its disregard for Constitutional authority.

> *Mr. Speaker, I have as much respect for the memory of the deceased, and as much sympathy for the sufferings of the living, if suffering there be, as any man in this House, but we must not permit our respect for the dead or our sympathy for a part of the living to lead us into*

an act of injustice to the balance of the living. I will not go into an argument to prove that Congress has no power to appropriate this money as an act of charity. Every member upon this floor knows it. We have the right, as individuals, to give away as much of our own money as we please in charity, but as members of Congress we have no right to appropriate a dollar of the public money.

Some eloquent appeals have been made to us upon the ground that this is a debt due the deceased. Mr Speaker, the deceased lived long after the close of the war, he was in office to the day of his death, and I have never heard that the government was in arrears to him. This government owes no debts but for services rendered, and at a stipulated price. If it is a debt, how much is it? Has it been audited, and the amount due ascertained? If it is a debt, this is not the place to present it for payment, or to have its merits examined. If it is a debt, we owe more than we can ever hope to pay, for we owe the widow of every soldier who fought in the War of 1812, precisely the same amount. . . . Sir, this is no debt. The government did not owe it to the deceased when he was alive; it could not contract it after he died.

. . .I do not wish to be rude, but I must be plain. Every man in this house knows it is not a debt. We cannot, without the grossest corruption, appropriate this money as the payment of a debt. We have not the semblance of authority to appropriate it as a charity. Mr. Speaker, I have said we have the right to give as much of our own money as we please. I am the poorest man on this floor. I cannot vote for the bill, but I will give one week's pay to the object, and if every member of Congress will do the same, it will amount to more than the bill asks.[11]

Compare Crockett's argument with the millions expended today for every social (charitable) program that can be conceived in federal minds. Does anyone think Crockett would have volunteers to answer his request for a week's pay from today's Congress? Every financial ill in the nation today can be laid at the door of government charity in the form of "entitlements" that are granted without a jot or tittle of Constitutional authority.

The time comes when an entity becomes so corrupted that reformation is impossible. That was true of religion in the dark ages and it is true of the "democracy" that supplanted America's Republic of sovereign States. The federal government cannot be reformed, nor can the Republic be restored upon the sinking sands of an entitlement-oriented, politically corrupt cesspool, swirling in Washington City. Today's federal government is a sordid mutation of the American Republic a political Frankenstein's monster, assembled from the Republic's rotting corpse. Created by the political/industrial complex of New England Republicans, that monster now stalks our land sucking flesh from the bones of American taxpayers. The only hope for our children and grandchildren—which none of them, and few others, comprehend—is secession and the reestablishment of our Constitutional Republic upon the rock-solid foundation of State sovereignty. Nothing less will return government to the intent of the Founders.

"The Greatest Generation" accelerated the destruction of State sovereignty when they went to Congress, occupied the White House and sat on the U. S. Supreme Court bench. In their campaign to create a world to insulate their children from life's realities, they imposed on us the "Fair Deal," the "New Frontier," and the "Great Society." In the process, they added tax burdens in the form of Medicare, enforcement of the so-called "Civil Rights Law," the busing of children across school districts, gerrymandering of Congressional districts, and "Affirmative Action," all in order to achieve "racial balance." By the 1990s, their offspring opened the flood gates of illegal immigration and gave us "cultural diversity" by which the country has devolved into a patchwork of "communities" resembling Baltic States and Banana Republics. Now they tell us we must embrace all cultures except the culture of America's last true Republic—the Confederate States.

In their war against Southern culture, they rewrote history and created a national mythology around the cult of Lincoln. Keenly aware of the power of motion picture propaganda, their Hollywood allies joined the campaign. Motion pictures have been a propaganda staple from their earliest days. Sergei Eisenstein first perfected the medium for propaganda in the wake of the Bolshevik Revolution. With a vastly illiterate population in the Soviet Republics, Eisenstein provided the Communists a tool for indoctrinating the masses and consolidating Bolshevik power. The people could not read, but they could view propaganda films that appealed to their emotions, which he cranked out in a constant torrent. Nazi Propaganda Minister, Heinrich Himmler, greatly admired Eisenstein's techniques and adopted them for Hitler's Third Reich. Among the great classic propaganda films is Leni Riefenstahl's "Triumph of The Will" that documented Hitler's Munich Rally, portraying him as the "Messiah" of the German people.

Motion pictures are designed to evoke emotions—a response that eliminates reason and critical thinking. The children of "The Greatest Generation" have given us powerfully orchestrated films to portray Southern depravity, demean America's heritage, and promote a socialist agenda.

Modern history books, written by children of "The Greatest Generation" and mandated in government schools, portray the Southern cause of sovereignty and self-government as racist. Through so-called "public education," generations of school children—even those in the South—have been brainwashed into accepting that label without question. General Cleburne's assessment of the aftermath of Southern defeat proved to be correct: "The history of this heroic struggle will be written by the enemy . . . our youth will be trained by Northern school teachers; will learn from Northern school books their version of the war." Few of today's school children—grandchildren and great-grandchildren of the "Greatest Generation"—understand the concept of State sovereignty. Neither State sovereignty nor the true history of Americans' struggle for liberty by America's truly Greatest Generation—the Founding Fathers—is taught in government schools. Wave upon wave of cell phone-wielding, texting, video game-playing, music down-loading, whining, narcissistic, highly self-esteemed students are shuttled through today's government schools ignorant of our founding documents and the former Republic that rested upon them.

What Hitler did in Germany has now reached fruition in America. Roosevelt and Hitler met in the American election of 2008. That election brought Americans to the valley of decision by turning the White House over to a person without qualifications for the presidency, whose goal is an American socialist state, and whose nationality remains at issue.

At the center of this accelerating descent into socialism is the Socialist/Democrat Party that now controls both the White House and the United States Congress. Its national leaders, platform, and flock of political sheep embrace and promote a political philosophy that is anti-Constitution. In that posture the Socialist/Democrat Party is both anti-American and traitorous to the United States. Not only is the Socialist/Democrat party committed to destroying private industry through nationalizing the banking, auto, and home mortgage industries, but it is now committed to socialized medicine.

Modern Republicans fare only slightly better than Socialist/Democrats in preserving individual liberty. It was a Republican—Lincoln—who destroyed State sovereignty and gave the nation corporate welfare. Because of Republican corporate welfare policies (Clay's "internal improvements") between 1861 and 1929, the nation suffered financial collapse. As a cure for the depressed nation, Roosevelt's federal programs of welfare for the poor proved worse than its illness. He simply brought another class into the fold of federal patronage that is perpetuated to this day.

The single redeeming quality of the Republican Party has been its ultimate metamorphosis, in recent years, from a party of big business into a small voice advocating sovereignty.

In 1968, Alabama Governor George Wallace ran for president on the American Party ticket. His candidacy gave voters a clear choice between his platform of State sovereignty and those of the Republicans and Democrats, whom he called, "Tweedle-Dee and Tweedle-Dum." Wallace was right when he said, "There's not a dime's worth of difference between Democrats and Republicans." From the 1820s onward, party politics gradually became the focus of the electoral process, relegating sovereignty to a lesser priority for American voters. As the political party system developed, each of them inevitably studied and analyzed the other's success. That led to each copying and using the other's promises of welfare to garner electoral support until by the mid-1900s the two major parties were as Wallace described them. The Republican Party was the party of corporate welfare and the Socialist/Democrat Party was the party of welfare for the poor— "Tweedle-Dee and Tweedle-Dum." Since Roosevelt instituted his "New Deal," the two major parties have waged a class warfare for votes, pitting the poor against the rich. Neither concerned itself with State sovereignty, but chose to perpetuate itself in power by purchasing votes with federal spending.

The outcome does not have to be the same in 21st century America. Jefferson Davis said, "The contest is not over, the strife is not ended. It has only entered upon a new and enlarged arena, and the principle for which we contend is bound to reassert itself, though it may at another time and in another form." Without realizing the relationship their actions bore to the principle for which the South contended, Americans who gathered for "Tea Parties" in 2009 to protest taxation for corporate bailouts reasserted Davis' principle of State sovereignty. There are enough unreconstructed Southerners and fellow conservatives across the land to again sound the tocsin of that principle, but the time for action is growing short.

There is no new thing under the sun. Patrick Henry's questions to his fellow delegates in 1775 remain as relevant today as they were then:

> *They tell us, sir, that we are weak—unable to cope with so formidable an adversary. But when shall we be stronger? Will it be the next week, or the next year? Will it be when we are totally disarmed? . . . Shall we gather strength by irresolution and inaction? Shall we acquire the means of effectual resistance by lying supinely on our backs, and hugging the delusive phantom of hope, until our enemies shall have bound us hand and foot?*[12]

His questions should engage the mind of every American who loves liberty. How long, America? Will we act only after "we are totally disarmed?" With a presumed president openly opposing gun ownership by private citizens, the federal government will continue to assault our Second Amendment right to keep and bear arms. The Founders included that provision to deter government tyranny. A disarmed citizenry is at the mercy of tyrants and disarmament is the first step tyrants take to subjugate a people. The Second Amendment was not included to protect hunters' rights—though it does that. It was meant to protect individual sovereignty against government tyranny.

What are Americans to do? We are the first generation in 148 years to be confronted with this situation. "What shall we do?"

The pattern for action is writ large across the pages of American history. We need to cut our political cloth from the Founders' pattern. They severed their ties with Britain and declared, "that these united colonies are, and of right out to be free and independent States." Washington's failure to protect State sovereignty constitutes a state of war that now exists between the federal government and the States. In response to that, those sovereign States should, and must if we are to remain free, declare, as Arkansas did in 1861, that, each of them "hereby resumes to herself all rights and powers heretofore delegated to the United States of America." Only in secession can individual liberty be vouchsafed to our children.

Americans continue to voice their discontent with federal programs across the land. The internet remains abuzz with the same rumblings, but Americans' anger has no effect on Washington politicians who turn a deaf ear to them and forge ahead with their Socialist agenda. A November 2009 National Rasmussen poll indicated that 71 percent of Americans surveyed were "somewhat angry with the policies of the federal government." That number included 46 percent who said they were "very angry."[13]

The solution many Americans offer for correcting federal tyranny—"vote the bums out"—simply won't work because of the great political divide between the States. For instance, Oklahoma has one of the most conservative Congressional delegations in Congress. Oklahoma's two conservative United States Senators, James Inhofe and Tom Coburn, wage relentless battles in behalf of Constitutional government, and all five of Oklahoma's United States Representatives are conservative— even the State's single Democrat Congressman. Barack Obama did not carry a single Oklahoma county in the 2008 presidential election nor would the overwhelming majority of Oklahoma voters keep Barney Frank, Harry Reid, Nancy Pelosi and their Socialist/Democrat cabal in office. The problem with the federal government is that voters in liberal States like Massachusetts,

California, Illinois, and New York will reelect their Socialist/Democrat representatives. Because such States have larger populations, the smaller States are in the same position of the smaller ones in 1787 who feared the loss of their sovereignty to a federal government dominated by larger States.

For small States who value their sovereignty, it isn't enough to simply say, "vote the bums out." Anger with the federal government is understandable, but elections will not change the government as long as large States continue to send anti-constitutionalists to represent them. The foundation of the Republic was State sovereignty. Small States have no voice in sister States' elections and cannot, therefore, rely on those States to preserve their sovereignty. That must come from the States themselves, not the federal government.

The only political figures who need to be involved in the current movement are State legislators who will reassert States' rights, not those who are only interested in co-opting a base of support for a political party. The Washington cesspool can never be reformed from the top down. If it is to be changed, that must come from the bottom up—the States acting through their sovereign people.

How long, America? How long will we allow Washington elitists to violate their oaths of office and sweep away the last vestiges of our liberty? Colonials had their "Tea Party" and addressed their grievances to Parliament but, like modern politicians, Parliament ignored them and pursued its own agenda. Acting in their sovereign capacities, the Colonists responded with fortitude and declared their separation from Britain. Eighty-five years later the Southern States objected to Constitutional usurpations by the federal government and that government ignored them. Like their Colonial sires, the South also responded with fortitude declaring its separation from the union.

America has addressed its grievances to Congress, receiving only contemptuous snorts in return. What will modern Americans do in the valley of decision? Will they simply object until they are silenced and meekly accept the loss of their liberties? Will they knuckle under to Washington elitists or will they do what must be done to preserve their liberty?

Patrick Henry told his fellow delegates, "I know of no way of judging the future but by the past. And judging by the past, I wish to know what there has been in the conduct of the British ministry for the last ten years, to justify those hopes with which gentlemen have been pleased to solace themselves and the House?" Translating Henry's sentiments into modern parlance, we ask, "What has there been in the conduct of the federal government over the last five decades to justify any hope that it will shrink and relinquish the powers it has stolen from the States?" To those who are mollified by the insidious smiles and warm greetings of Washington elitists, Patrick Henry says, "Trust it not, sir; it will prove a snare to your feet. Suffer not yourselves to be betrayed with a kiss. Ask yourselves how this gracious reception of our petition comports with these warlike preparations which cover our waters and darken our land."[14]

After all has been said and done in "Tea Parties," rallies, and Congressional Town Hall Meetings, Congress continues to pursue its own agenda, turn a deaf ear to those whom it represents, increase their taxes and trample their liberties underfoot. What is the course to be taken? Will Americans surrender a little more of their liberty, hoping all will work out in the end? Will they say, "Maybe things will get better?" Patrick Henry would say,

> *Sir, we have done everything that could be done to avert the storm which is now coming on. We have petitioned;*

> *we have remonstrated; we have supplicated; we have prostrated ourselves before the throne, and have implored its interposition to arrest the tyrannical hands of the ministry and Parliament.*
>
> *Our petitions have been slighted; our remonstrances have produced additional violence and insult; our supplications have been disregarded; and we have been spurned, with contempt, from the foot of the throne. In vain, after these things, may we indulge the fond hope of peace and reconciliation. There is no longer any room for hope.*[15]

The petitions, remonstrances, and supplications of American voters have been "slighted" and answered with "additional violence and insult." Washington ceased any meaningful dialogue between itself and the voters long ago and ended "any room for hope." How long, America? Are there any Americans left with the courage of our Fathers who will tell their State legislators they've had enough and it's time to leave? Are there enough patriotic Americans in State legislatures to do what the colonists did in 1776 to rid themselves of tyranny? Is there a Patrick Henry among the States today?

If the great principles upon which our Republic was founded are to be transmitted unshorn to our children, time is of the essence. Another generation of federal business-as-usual will eradicate every last vestige of American liberty. Patrick Henry says if we are to remain free, we must act now.

> *The battle, sir, is not to the strong alone; it is to the vigilant, the active, the brave. Besides, sir, we have no election. If we were base enough to desire it, it is now too late to retire from the contest. There is no retreat but in submission and slavery! Our chains are forged!*

It is in vain, sir, to extenuate the matter. Gentlemen may cry 'Peace! Peace!' - - but there is no peace. The war is actually begun! The next gale that sweeps from the north will bring to our ears the clash of resounding arms. . . What is it that gentlemen wish? What would they have? Is life so dear, or peace so sweet, as to be purchased at the price of chains and slavery? Forbid it, Almighty God! I know not what course others may take; but as for me, give me liberty, or give me death![16]

The majority of those who demonstrated in "Tea Parties" and voiced their objections to federal usurpation of States' Rights in 2009 probably do not know who Jefferson Davis was, but they were doing what he predicted. State sovereignty was the principle to which Davis referred when he said, "The contest is not over, the strife is not ended. It has only entered upon a new and enlarged arena, and the principle for which we contend is bound to reassert itself, though it may be at another time and in another form."[17] Unknown to them, those voices raised across America against the Washington regime are echoing the principle of State sovereignty which the Confederate States defended from 1861 to 1865. Like a great Phoenix rising from the ashes of Lincoln's war, that principle is stirring in our States. The 2016 election may have been the sound of its rustling wings. Only time will tell.

The single remnant of the American Republic that remains is the sovereignty of the people of the States. Though all else should be taken from us, that God-given right will always remain and the only thing that can prevent us from reclaiming our States' sovereignty is a lack of individual will.

It is time to choose. If Americans truly are heirs to the Jeffersonian legacy, then it has always been and must always be, not only our right, but our duty as citizens to withdraw consent from any government that becomes destructive of life, liberty, or the pursuit of happiness.

If, however, *We the People* believe ourselves incompetent to judge when that line has been crossed, then we will continue to find no shortage of political masters eager to carry on Lincoln's legacy of contempt for our Constitution, and violent suppression of self-government.

Either way, one thing is certain: America will never regain the principles of her founding until her people muster the courage and clarity to finally separate liberty's friends from its foes.[18]

Two roads lie before us in the valley of decision. There is no middle ground. We either take the high road and reclaim our sovereignty, or we shuffle silently down the low road in chains of federal tyranny. To do the latter will surrender what is left of our liberty and bequeath our own political fetters to our children. Do we have the will to secede and reclaim our sovereignty? The signers of the Declaration of Independence did. The choice is ours. How long, America?

---

[1] Correspondence between Lord John Dalberg Acton and Robert E. Lee, 1866.

[2] *Ibid.*

[3] James A Garfield, Inaugural Address, March 4, 1881.

[4] Dr. John W. Baer, "The Pledge of Allegiance, A Short History," 1992, from http://www.oldtimeislands.org/pledge/pledge.htm

[5] President James Madison, First Inaugural Address, March 4, 1809.

⁶ President Andrew Jackson, First Inaugural Address, March 4, 1829.

⁷ "Feds Back Off Threat to Pull Funds Over English-Only Law; OK Delegation Reacts," *The Elk City Daily News*, Elk City, Okla., Oct. 9, 2009, p. 8.

⁸ *Ibid.*

⁹ *Ibid.*

¹⁰ *Ibid.*

¹¹ Congressman David Crockett, speech in the U. S. House of Representatives, April 1828. Some scholars question the authenticity of this speech, but debate on the proposal to grant a charitable contribution to General Brown's widow can be found in "U. S. Congressional Documents and Debates, 1774-1875," at http://memory.loc.gov.

¹² Patrick Henry, Speech in the Virginia House of Burgesses, March 23, 1775.

¹³ http://tinyurl.com/rasmussen-71pc-angry-at-govt

¹⁴ Patrick Henry, Speech, March 23, 1775.

¹⁵ *Ibid.*

¹⁶ *Ibid.*

¹⁷ Jefferson Davis, Speech to Mississippi Legislature, 1871.

¹⁸ Josh Esboch, "Jefferson vs Lincoln: America Must Choose," Feb. 20, 2010, www.tenthamendmentcenter.com/2010/02/20/jefferson-vs-lincoln-america-must-choose/

Appendix A

THE FOLLOWING is a comparison between the United States Constitution, written in 1787, and the Constitution of the Confederate States of America, written and adopted in 1861. This is taken from Jefferson Davis' work, *The Rise and Fall of The Confederate Government*, published in 1889.

United States Constitution, Preamble: We the People of the United States, in order to form a more perfect Union, establish Justice, insure domestic Tranquillity, provide for the common defence, promote the general Welfare, and secure the Blessings of Liberty to ourselves and our Posterity, do ordain and establish this Constitution for the United States of America.

Confederate States Constitution, Preamble: We, the People of the Confederate States, each State acting in its sovereign and independent character, in order to form a permanent Federal Government, establish justice, insure domestic tranquility, and secure the blessings of liberty to ourselves and our posterity—invoking the favor and guidance of Almighty God—do ordain and establish this Constitution for the Confederate States of America.

U.S: The House of Representatives shall chuse their Speaker and other officers; and shall have the sole Power of Impeachment.

C.S.: The House of Representatives shall choose their Speaker and other officers; and shall have the sole power of impeachment, except that any judicial or other Federal officer, resident and acting solely within the limits of any State, may be impeached by a vote of two thirds of both branches of the Legislature thereof.

U.S.: No Senator or Representative shall, during the time for which he was elected, be appointed to any civil Office under the Authority of the United States, which shall have been created, or the Emoluments whereof shall have been increased during such time; and no Person holding any Office under the United States, shall be a Member of either House during his Continuance in Office.

C.S.: No Senator or Representative shall, during the time for which he was elected, be appointed to any civil office under the authority of the Confederate States, which shall have been created, or the emoluments whereof shall have been increased during such time; and no person holding any office under the Confederate States, shall be a member of either House during his continuance in office. But Congress may, by law, grant to the principal officer in each of the executive departments a seat upon the floor of either House, with the privilege of discussing any measures appertaining to his department.

U.S.: Every Bill which shall have passed the House of Representatives and the Senate, shall, before it become a Law, be presented to the President of the United States; If he approve he shall sign it, but if not he shall return it, with his Objections to that House in which it shall have originated, who shall enter the Objections at large on their Journal, and proceed to reconsider it. . . .

C.S.: Every bill which shall have passed both Houses, shall, before it becomes a law, be presented to the President of the Confederate States; if he approve, he shall sign it; but if not, he shall return it, with his objections, to that House in which it shall have originated, who shall enter the objections at large on their journal, and proceed to reconsider it. . . . The President may approve any appropriation and disapprove any other appropriation in the same bill. In such case he shall, in signing the bill, designate the appropriations disapproved; and shall return a copy of such appropriations, with his objections, to the House in which the bill shall have originated; and the same proceedings shall then be had as in case of other bills disapproved by the President.

U.S.: The Congress shall have Power to lay and collect Taxes, Duties, Imposts and Excises, to pay the Debts and provide for the common Defence and general Welfare of the United States; but all Duties, Imposts and Excises shall be uniform throughout the United States;

C.S.: The Congress shall have power to lay and collect taxes, duties, imposts, and excises, for revenue necessary to pay the debts, provide for the common defense, and carry on the Government of the Confederate States; but no bounties shall be granted from the Treasury; nor shall any duties or taxes on importations from foreign nations be laid to promote or foster any branch of industry; and all duties, imposts, and excises shall be uniform throughout the Confederate States;

U.S.: To regulate Commerce with foreign Nations, and among the several States, and with the Indian Tribes;

C.S.: To regulate commerce with foreign nations, and among the several States, and with the Indian tribes; but neither this, nor any other clause contained in the Constitution, shall ever be construed to delegate the power to Congress to appropriate money for any internal improvement intended to facilitate commerce; except for the purpose of furnishing lights, beacons, and buoys, and other aid to navigation upon the coasts, and the improvement of harbors and the removing of obstructions in river navigation, in all which cases, such duties shall be laid on the navigation facilitated thereby, as may be necessary to pay the costs and expenses thereof;

U.S.: To establish an uniform Rule of Naturalization, and uniform Laws on the subject of Bankruptcies throughout the United States;

C.S.: To establish uniform laws of naturalization, and uniform laws on the subject of bankruptcies, throughout the Confederate States; but no law of Congress shall discharge any debt contracted before the passage of the same;

U.S.: To establish Post Offices and post roads;

C.S.: To establish post-offices and post routes; but the expenses of the Post-Office Department, after the first day of March, in the year of our Lord eighteen hundred and sixty-three, shall be paid out of its own revenue;

U.S.: The Migration or Importation of such Persons as any of the States now existing shall think proper to admit, shall not be prohibited by the Congress prior to the Year one thousand eight hundred and eight, but a Tax or Duty may be imposed on such Importation, and not exceeding ten dollars for each Person.

C.S.: The importation of negroes of the African race, from any foreign country other than the slave-holding States or Territories of the United States of America, is hereby forbidden; and Congress is required to pass such laws as shall effectually prevent the same. Congress shall also have power to prohibit the introduction of slaves from any State not a member of, or Territory not belonging to, this Confederacy.

U.S.: No Tax or Duty shall be laid on Articles exported from any State.

C.S.: No tax or duty shall be laid on articles exported from any State except by a vote of two-thirds of both houses.

U.S.: ....

C.S.: Every law, or resolution having the force of law, shall relate to but one subject, and that shall be expressed in the title.

U.S.: No State shall, without the Consent of Congress, lay any Duty of Tonnage, keep Troops, or Ships of War in time of Peace, enter into any Agreement or Compact with another State, or with a foreign Power, or engage in War, unless actually invaded, or in such imminent Danger as will not admit of Delay.

C.S.: No State shall, without the consent of Congress, lay any duty on tonnage, except on sea-going vessels for the improvement of its rivers and harbors navigated by the said vessels; but such duties shall not conflict with any treaties of the Confederate States with foreign nations. And any surplus revenue thus derived shall, after making such improvement, be paid into the common Treasury; nor shall any State keep troops or ships of war in time of peace, enter into any agreement of compact with another State, or with a foreign power, or engage in war unless actually invaded, or in such imminent danger as will not admit of delay. But when any river divides or flows through two or more States, they may enter into compacts with each other to improve the navigation thereof.

U.S.: The executive Power shall be vested in a President of the United States of America. He shall hold his Office during the Term of four Years, and, together with the Vice President, chosen for the same Term, be elected, as follows:

C.S.: The executive Power shall be vested in a President of the Confederate States of America. He and the Vice-President shall hold their offices for the term of six years; but the President shall not be reëligible. The President and the Vice-President shall be elected as follows:

U.S.: . . . .

C.S.: The principal officer in each of the executive departments, and all persons connected with the diplomatic service, may be removed from office at the pleasure of the President. All other civil officers of the executive department may be removed at any time by the President, or other appointing power, when their services are unnecessary, or for dishonesty, incapacity, inefficiency, misconduct, or neglect of duty; and, when so removed the removal shall be reported to the Senate, together with the reasons therefore.

U.S.: The President shall have Power to fill up all Vacancies that may happen during the Recess of the Senate, by granting Commissions which shall expire at the End of their next Session

C.S.: The President shall have power to fill up all vacancies that may happen during the recess of the Senate, by granting commissions which shall expire at the end of their next session. But no person rejected by the Senate shall be reappointed to the same office during their ensuing recess.

U.S.: The judicial Power shall extend to all Cases, in Law and Equity, arising under this Constitution, the Laws of the United States, and Treaties made, or which shall be made, under their Authority;—to all Cases affecting Ambassadors, other public Ministers and Consuls;—to all Cases of admiralty and maritime Jurisdiction;—to Controversies to which the United States shall be a Party;—to Controversies between two or more States;—between a State and Citizens of another State;—between Citizens of different States,—between Citizens of the same State claiming Lands under Grants of different States, and between a State, or the Citizens thereof, and foreign States, Citizens or Subjects.

C.S.: The judicial power shall extend to all cases arising under this Constitution, the laws of the Confederate States, and treaties made, or which shall be made, under their authority; to all cases affecting ambassadors, other public ministers, and consuls; to all cases of admiralty and maritime jurisdiction; to controversies to which the Confederate States shall be a party; to controversies between two or more States; between a State and citizens of another State, where the State is plaintiff; between citizens claiming lands under grants of different States, and between a State or the citizens thereof, and foreign states, citizens, or subjects. But no State shall be sued by a citizen or subject of any foreign state.

U.S.: The Citizens of each State shall be entitled to all Privileges and Immunities of Citizens in the several States.

C.S.: The citizens of each State shall be entitled to all the privileges and immunities of citizens in the several States, and shall have the right of transit and sojourn in any State of this Confederacy, with their slaves and other property; and the right of property in said slaves shall not be thereby impaired.

U.S.: No Person held to Service or Labour in one State, under the Laws thereof, escaping into another, shall, in Consequence of any Law or Regulation therein, be discharged from such Service or Labour, but shall be delivered up on Claim of the Party to whom such Service or Labour may be due.

C.S.: No slave or other person held to service or labor in any State or Territory of the Confederate States, under the laws thereof, escaping or lawfully carried into another, shall, in consequence of any law or regulation therein, be discharged from such service or labor; but shall be delivered up on claim of the party to whom such slave belongs, or to whom such service or labor may be due.

U.S.: New States may be admitted by the Congress into this Union; but no new State shall be formed or erected within the Jurisdiction of any other State; nor any State be formed by the Junction of two or more States, or Parts of States, without the

Consent of the Legislatures of the States concerned as well as of the Congress.

C.S.: Other States may be admitted into this Confederacy by a vote of two thirds of the whole House of Representatives and two thirds of the Senate, the Senate voting by States; but no new State shall be formed or erected within the jurisdiction of any other State; nor any State be formed by the junction of two or more States, or parts of States, without the consent of the Legislatures of the States concerned, as well as of the Congress.

The Confederate States may acquire new territory; and Congress shall have power to legislate and provide governments for the inhabitants of all territory belonging to the Confederate States, lying without the limits of the several States; and may permit them, at such times and in such manner as it may by law provide, to form States to be admitted into the Confederacy. In all such territory, the institution, of negro slavery, as it now exists in the Confederate States, shall be recognized and protected by Congress and by the territorial government; and the inhabitants of the several Confederate States and Territories shall have the right to take to such Territory any slaves lawfully held by them in any of the States or Territories of the Confederate States.

U.S.: The Congress, whenever two-thirds of both Houses shall deem it necessary, shall propose Amendments to this Constitution, or, on the Application of the Legislatures of two-thirds of the several States, shall call a Convention for proposing Amendments, which, in either Case, shall be valid to all Intents and Purposes, as Part of this Constitution, when ratified by the Legislatures of three-fourths of the several States, or by

Conventions in three-fourths thereof, as the one or the other Mode of Ratification may be proposed by the Congress:

C.S.: Upon the demand of any three States, legally assembled in their several conventions, the Congress shall summon a Convention of all the States, to take into consideration such amendments to the Constitution as the said States shall concur in suggesting at the time when the said demand is made; and should any of the proposed amendments to the Constitution be agreed on by the said Convention—voting by States—and the same be ratified by the Legislatures of two thirds of the several States, or by conventions in two-thirds thereof—as the one or the other mode of ratification may be proposed by the general Convention—they shall thenceforward form a part of this Constitution.

U.S.: The enumeration in the Constitution, of certain rights, shall not be construed to deny or disparage others retained by the people.

C.S.: The enumeration, in the Constitution, of certain rights, shall not be construed to deny or disparage others retained by the people of the several States.

Stripping State Legislative Sovereignty

States were further stripped of their sovereignty by the 17th Amendment to the Constitution, passed by a Republican Congress on May 31, 1912, and ratified on April 8, 1913. That destroyed the compromise between smaller and larger states over representation in the Congress and repealed the right of state legislatures to appoint their U. S. Senators. The diffusion of constituencies, mandated in the Constitution of 1787, was eliminated. The States lost their sovereign voices in the federal government and the Republic was mutated into a "democracy."

> *The Senate of the United States shall be composed of two Senators from each state, elected by the people thereof, for six years; and each Senator shall have one vote. The electors in each state shall have the qualifications requisite for electors of the most numerous branch of the state legislatures*
>
> *When vacancies happen in the representation of any State in the Senate, the executive authority of such State shall issue writs of election to fill such vacancies: Provided, That the legislature of any State may empower the executive authority to make temporary appointments until the people fill the vacancies by election as the legislature may direct.*
>
> *This amendment shall not be so construed as to affect the election or term of any Senator chosen before it becomes valid as part of the Constitution.*

The reason for two legislative bodies in the United States Congress was so sovereign State governments would have national voices through Senators appointed by them. By eliminating the provision whereby Senators were appointed by the legislatures, this amendment rendered a bicameral Congress superfluous. With Senators elected by popular vote in State elections, this amendment means that each State is now actually represented by two additional Congressmen—those elected in districts drawn within the States and two Senators elected at-large. The 17th Amendment eliminated any practical need for two houses of Congress, silenced the voice of State governments and removed another vestige of State sovereignty.

With the passage of the 17th Amendment, a "tyranny of the majority" that the Founders sought to avoid was brought closer to reality. Neither the signers of the Declaration of Independence, the men who fought the War for Independence, nor the Framers of the Constitution intended to establish a democracy. Patrick Henry did *not* say, "Give me democracy or give me death!"

One remnant of the Republic's elective processes—the Electoral College—remains intact, but its repeal is constantly being urged. The Electoral College was designed as a buffer against a "tyranny of the majority" in the Republic and as a safeguard to ensure State sovereignty. The Constitution specified that the president should be elected by electors which, "Each State shall appoint, in such Manner as the legislature thereof may direct." State legislatures have sole authority in determining how the electors of their States shall be selected and from the beginning most legislatures chose the electors themselves.

In the first election in 1789 only ten States took part in electing George Washington. North Carolina and Rhode Island had not yet ratified the Constitution. Of those ten, only the Maryland, Pennsylvania and Virginia legislatures opted to choose presidential electors in their States by popular vote. In the second presidential election of 1792 there were fifteen States who participated, but only five of them selected presidential electors by popular vote. By 1816 just over half of the States selected their electors by popular vote, and in 1828 only two State legislatures—Delaware and South Carolina—selected their electors. The trend toward selecting presidential electors by popular vote continued until all of the States adopted that method in 1876. While selecting presidential electors by popular vote is an option for legislatures, they have surrendered a great deal of their sovereignty through that method. There is nothing to prevent modern State legislatures from selecting the presidential electors themselves without a popular vote. This is one Constitutional avenue to reclaim the sovereignty that has been stolen from them and to prevent the "tyranny of the majority" from voting solely for government handouts. The Founders established a representative Republic, not a direct democracy. The Electoral College must be kept intact. If it is ever abolished the American Republic will finally be relegated to the ash heap of history.

The things we have delineated in this chapter were foretold more than two centuries ago in the first "Anti-Federalist Paper." Listing what the writer called the "uncontroulable powers" of Congress, he concluded by saying, "they may so exercise this power as entirely to annihilate all state governments...and if they may do it, it is pretty certain they will; for it will be found that the power retained by the individual states, small as it is, will be a clog upon the wheels of the government of the united states; the latter therefore will be naturally inclined to remove it out of the way." Because of men like Hamilton, Clay, Lincoln, and their political heirs, today's States have become vassals of the federal government.

Appendix B

THAT SLAVERY was an issue between North and South in 1860 is not to be denied. That slavery was the sole cause of secession and the consequent war waged upon the South by Lincoln is false. To eliminate States' rights and institute a centralized government over free people, Lincoln offered slavery as the reason for his war. To do the same thing today, the federal government offers welfare and a "War on Terrorism" as its reason. As proof of that, we offer these secession ordinances that delineate and document the Constitutional usurpations leading to each State's secession.

South Carolina Secession Ordinance

AN ORDINANCE to dissolve the union between the State of South Carolina and other States united with her under the compact entitled "The Constitution of the United States of America."

We, the people of the State of South Carolina, in convention assembled, do declare and ordain, and it is hereby declared and ordained, That the ordinance adopted by us in convention on the twenty-third day of May, in the year of our Lord one thousand seven hundred and eighty-eight, whereby the Constitution of the United States of America was ratified, and also all acts and parts of acts of the General Assembly of this State ratifying amendments of the said Constitution, are hereby repealed; and that the union now subsisting between South Carolina and other States, under the name of the "United States of America," is hereby dissolved.

Done at Charleston the twentieth day of December, in the year of our Lord one thousand eight hundred and sixty.

Virginia Secession Ordinance

AN ORDINANCE

To Repeal the ratification of the Constitution of the United States of America, by the State of Virginia, and to resume all the rights and powers granted under said Constitution:

The people of Virginia, in their ratification of the Constitution of the United States of America, adopted by them in Convention, on the 25th day of June, in the year of our Lord one thousand seven hundred and eight-eight, having declared that the powers granted them under the said Constitution were derived from the people of the United States, and might be resumed whensoever the same should be perverted to their injury and oppression, and the Federal Government having perverted said powers, not only to the injury of the people of Virginia, but to the oppression of the Southern slaveholding States.

Now, therefore, we, the people of Virginia, do declare and ordain that the Ordinance adopted by the people of this State in Convention, on the twenty-fifth day of June, in the year of our Lord one thousand seven hundred and seventy-eight, whereby the Constitution of the United States of America was ratified, and all acts of the General Assembly of this State, ratifying or adopting amendments to said Constitution, are hereby repealed and abrogated; that the union between the State of Virginia and the other States under the Constitution aforesaid, is hereby dissolved, and that the State of Virginia is in the full possession and exercise of all the rights of sovereignty which belong to a free and independent State. And they do further declare that the said Constitution of the United State of America is no longer binding on any of the citizens of this State.

This Ordinance shall take effect and be an act of this day when ratified by a majority of the votes of the people of this State, cast at a poll to be taken thereon on the fourth Thursday in May next, in pursuance of a schedule hereafter to be enacted.

Done in Convention, in the city of Richmond, on the seventeenth day of April, in the year of our Lord one thousand eight hundred and sixty-one, and in the eighty-fifth year of the Commonwealth of Virginia.

Mississippi Secession Ordinance

AN ORDINANCE to dissolve the union between the State of Mississippi and other States united with her under the compact entitled "The Constitution of the United States of America."

The people of the State of Mississippi, in convention assembled, do ordain and declare, and it is hereby ordained and declared, as follows, to wit:

Section 1. That all the laws and ordinances by which the said State of Mississippi became a member of the Federal Union of the United States of America be, and the same are hereby, repealed, and that all obligations on the part of the said State or the people thereof to observe the same be withdrawn, and that the said State doth hereby resume all the rights, functions, and powers which by any of said laws or ordinances were conveyed to the Government of the said United States, and is absolved from all the obligations, restraints, and duties incurred to the said Federal Union, and shall from henceforth be a free, sovereign, and independent State.

Sec. 2. That so much of the first section of the seventh article of the constitution of this State as requires members of the Legislature and all officers, executive and judicial, to take an oath or affirmation to support the Constitution of the United States be, and the same is hereby, abrogated and annulled.

Sec. 3. That all rights acquired and vested under the Constitution of the United States, or under any act of Congress passed, or treaty made, in pursuance thereof, or under any law of this State, and not incompatible with this ordinance, shall remain in force and have the same effect as if this ordinance had not been passed.

Sec. 4. That the people of the State of Mississippi hereby consent to form a federal union with such of the States as may have seceded or may secede from the Union of the United States of America, upon the basis of the present Constitution of the said United States, except such parts thereof as embrace other portions than such seceding States.

Thus ordained and declared in convention the 9th day of January, in the year of our Lord 1861.

Florida Secession Ordinance

ORDINANCE OF SECESSION

We, the people of the State of Florida, in convention assembled, do solemnly ordain, publish, and declare, That the State of Florida hereby withdraws herself from the confederacy of States existing under the name of the United States of America and from the existing Government of the said States; and that all political connection between her and the Government of said States ought to be, and the same is hereby, totally annulled, and said Union of States dissolved; and the State of Florida is hereby declared a sovereign and independent nation; and that all ordinances heretofore adopted, in so far as they create or recognize said Union, are rescinded; and all laws or parts of laws in force in this State, in so far as they recognize or assent to said Union, be, and they are hereby, repealed. (Passed 10 Jan. 1861)

Alabama Secession Ordinance

AN ORDINANCE to dissolve the union between the State of Alabama and the other States united under the compact styled "The Constitution of the United States of America"

Whereas, the election of Abraham Lincoln and Hannibal Hamlin to the offices of president and vice-president of the United States of America, by a sectional party, avowedly hostile to the domestic institutions and to the peace and security of the people of the State of Alabama, preceded by many and dangerous infractions of the constitution of the United States by many of the States and people of the Northern section, is a political wrong of so insulting and menacing a character as to justify the people of the State of Alabama in the adoption of prompt and decided measures for their future peace and security, therefore:

Be it declared and ordained by the people of the State of Alabama, in Convention assembled, That the State of Alabama now withdraws, and is hereby withdrawn from the Union known as "the United States of America," and henceforth ceases to be one of said United States, and is, and of right ought to be a Sovereign and Independent State.

Sec 2. Be it further declared and ordained by the people of the State of Alabama in Convention assembled, That all powers over the Territory of said State, and over the people thereof, heretofore delegated to the Government of the United States of America, be and they are hereby withdrawn from said Government, and are hereby resumed and vested in the people of the State of Alabama. And as it is the desire and purpose of the people of Alabama to meet the slaveholding States of the South, who may approve such purpose, in order to frame a provisional as well as permanent Government upon the principles of the Constitution of the United States,

Be it resolved by the people of Alabama in Convention assembled, That the people of the States of Delaware, Maryland, Virginia, North Carolina, South Carolina, Florida, Georgia, Mississippi, Louisiana, Texas, Arkansas, Tennessee, Kentucky and Missouri, be and are hereby invited to meet the people of the State of Alabama, by their Delegates, in Convention, on the 4th day of February, A.D., 1861, at the city of Montgomery, in the State of Alabama, for the purpose of consulting with each other as to the most effectual mode of securing concerted and harmonious action in whatever measures may be deemed most desirable for our common peace and security.

And be it further resolved, That the President of this Convention, be and is hereby instructed to transmit forthwith a copy of the foregoing Preamble, Ordinance, and Resolutions to the Governors of the several States named in said resolutions.

Done by the people of the State of Alabama, in Convention assembled, at Montgomery, on this, the eleventh day of January, A.D. 1861.

Georgia Secession Ordinance

We the people of the State of Georgia in Convention assembled do declare and ordain and it is hereby declared and ordained that the ordinance adopted by the State of Georgia in convention on the 2nd day of Jany. in the year of our Lord seventeen hundred and eighty-eight, whereby the constitution of the United States of America was assented to, ratified and adopted, and also all acts and parts of acts of the general assembly of this State, ratifying and adopting amendments to said constitution, are hereby repealed, rescinded and abrogated.

We do further declare and ordain that the union now existing between the State of Georgia and other States under the name of the United States of America is hereby dissolved, and that the State of Georgia is in full possession and exercise of all those rights of sovereignty which belong and appertain to a free and independent State. Passed January 19, 1861.

Louisiana Secession Ordinance

AN ORDINANCE to dissolve the union between the State of Louisiana and other States united with her under the compact entitled "The Constitution of the United States of America."

We, the people of the State of Louisiana, in convention assembled, do declare and ordain, and it is hereby declared and ordained, That the ordinance passed by us in convention on the 22d day of November, in the year eighteen hundred and eleven, whereby the Constitution of the United States of America and the amendments of the said Constitution were adopted, and all laws and ordinances by which the State of Louisiana became a member of the Federal Union, be, and the same are hereby, repealed and abrogated; and that the union now subsisting between Louisiana and other States under the name of "The United States of America" is hereby dissolved.

We do further declare and ordain, That the State of Louisiana hereby resumes all rights and powers heretofore delegated to the Government of the United States of America; that her citizens are absolved from all allegiance to said Government; and that she is in full possession and exercise of all those rights of sovereignty which appertain to a free and independent State.

We do further declare and ordain, That all rights acquired and vested under the Constitution of the United States, or any act of Congress, or treaty, or under any law of this State, and not incompatible with this ordinance, shall remain in force and have the same effect as if this ordinance had not been passed.

Adopted in convention at Baton Rouge this 26th day of January, 1861.

Texas Secession Ordinance

AN ORDINANCE to dissolve the Union between the State of Texas and the other States united under the Compact styled "the Constitution of the United States of America."

WHEREAS, The Federal Government has failed to accomplish the purposes of the compact of union between these States, in giving protection either to the persons of our people upon an exposed frontier, or to the property of our citizens, and

WHEREAS, the action of the Northern States of the Union is violative of the compact between the States and the guarantees of the Constitution; and,

WHEREAS, The recent developments in Federal affairs make it evident that the power of the Federal Government is sought to be made a weapon with which to strike down the interests and property of the people of Texas, and her sister slave-holding States, instead of permitting it to be, as was intended, our shield against outrage and aggression; THEREFORE,

SECTION 1. We, the people of the State of Texas, by delegates in convention assembled, do declare and ordain that the ordinance adopted by our convention of delegates on the 4th day of July, A.D. 1845, and afterwards ratified by us, under which the Republic of Texas was admitted into the Union with other States, and became a party to the compact styled "The Constitution of the United States of America," be, and is hereby, repealed and annulled; that all the powers which, by the said compact, were delegated by Texas to the Federal Government are revoked and resumed; that Texas is of right absolved from all restraints and obligations incurred by said compact, and is a separate sovereign State, and that her citizens and people are absolved from all allegiance to the United States or the government thereof.

SEC. 2. This ordinance shall be submitted to the people of Texas for their ratification or rejection, by the qualified voters, on the 23rd day of February, 1861, and unless rejected by a majority of the votes cast, shall take effect and be in force on and after the 2d day of March, A.D. 1861.

PROVIDED, that in the Representative District of El Paso said election may be held on the 18th day of February, 1861.

Done by the people of the State of Texas, in convention assembled, at Austin, this 1st day of February, A.D. 1861.

Ratified 23 Feb 1861 by a vote of 46,153 for and 14,747 against

Arkansas Secession Ordinance

AN ORDINANCE to dissolve the union now existing between the State of Arkansas and the other States united with her under the compact entitled "The Constitution of the United States of America."

Whereas, in addition to the well-founded causes of complaint set forth by this convention, in resolutions adopted on the 11th of March, A.D. 1861, against the sectional party now in power in Washington City, headed by Abraham Lincoln, he has, in the face of resolutions passed by this convention pledging the State of Arkansas to resist to the last extremity any attempt on the part of such power to coerce any State that had seceded from the old Union, proclaimed to the world that war should be waged against such States until they should be compelled to submit to their rule, and large forces to accomplish this have by this same power been called out, and are now being marshaled to carry out this inhuman design; and to longer submit to such rule, or remain in the old Union of the United States, would be disgraceful and ruinous to the State of Arkansas:

Therefore we, the people of the State of Arkansas, in convention assembled, do hereby declare and ordain, and it is hereby declared and ordained, That the "ordinance and acceptance of compact" passed and approved by the General Assembly of the State of Arkansas on the 18th day of October, A.D. 1836, whereby it was by said General Assembly ordained that by virtue of the authority vested in said General Assembly by the provisions of the ordinance adopted by the convention of delegates assembled at Little Rock for the purpose of forming a constitution and system of government for said State, the propositions set forth in "An act supplementary to an act entitled 'An act for the admission of the State of Arkansas into the Union, and to provide for the due execution of the laws of the United States within the same, and for other purposes,'" were freely accepted, ratified, and irrevocably confirmed, articles of compact and union between the State of Arkansas and the United States, and all other laws and every other law and ordinance, whereby the State of Arkansas became a member of the Federal Union, be, and the same are hereby, in all respects and for every purpose herewith consistent, repealed, abrogated, and fully set aside; and the union now subsisting between the State of Arkansas and the other States, under the name of the United States of America, is hereby forever dissolved.

And we do further hereby declare and ordain, That the State of Arkansas hereby resumes to herself all rights and powers heretofore delegated to the Government of the United States of

America; that her citizens are absolved from all allegiance to said Government of the United States, and that she is in full possession and exercise of all the rights and sovereignty which appertain to a free and independent State.

We do further ordain and declare, That all rights acquired and vested under the Constitution of the United States of America, or of any act or acts of Congress, or treaty, or under any law of this State, and not incompatible with this ordinance, shall remain in full force and effect, in nowise altered or impaired, and have the same effect as if this ordinance had not been passed.

Adopted and passed in open convention on the 6th day of May, A.D. 1861.

North Carolina Secession Ordinance

AN ORDINANCE to dissolve the union between the State of North Carolina and the other States united with her, under the compact of government entitled "The Constitution of the United States."

We, the people of the State of North Carolina in convention assembled, do declare and ordain, and it is hereby declared and ordained, That the ordinance adopted by the State of North Carolina in the convention of 1789, whereby the Constitution of the United States was ratified and adopted, and also all acts and parts of acts of the General Assembly ratifying and adopting amendments to the said Constitution, are hereby repealed, rescinded, and abrogated.

We do further declare and ordain, That the union now subsisting between the State of North Carolina and the other States, under the title of the United States of America, is hereby dissolved, and that the State of North Carolina is in full possession and exercise of all those rights of sovereignty which belong and appertain to a free and independent State.

Done in convention at the city of Raleigh, this the 20th day of May, in the year of our Lord 1861, and in the eighty-fifth year of the independence of said State.

Tennessee Secession Ordinance

DECLARATION OF INDEPENDENCE AND ORDINANCE dissolving the federal relations between the State of Tennessee and the United States of America.

First. We, the people of the State of Tennessee, waiving any expression of opinion as to the abstract doctrine of secession, but asserting the right, as a free and independent people, to alter, reform, or abolish our form of government in such manner as we think proper, do ordain and declare that all the laws and ordinances by which the State of Tennessee became a member of the Federal Union of the United States of America are hereby abrogated and annulled, and that all the rights, functions, and powers which by any of said laws and ordinances were conveyed to the Government of the United States, and to absolve ourselves from all the obligations, restraints, and duties incurred thereto; and do hereby henceforth become a free, sovereign, and independent State.

Second. We furthermore declare and ordain that article 10, sections 1 and 2, of the constitution of the State of Tennessee, which requires members of the General Assembly and all officers, civil and military, to take an oath to support the Constitution of the United States be, and the same are hereby, abrogated and annulled, and all parts of the constitution of the State of Tennessee making citizenship of the United States a qualification for office and recognizing the Constitution of the

United States as the supreme law of this State are in like manner abrogated and annulled.

Third. We furthermore ordain and declare that all rights acquired and vested under the Constitution of the United States, or under any act of Congress passed in pursuance thereof, or under any laws of this State, and not incompatible with this ordinance, shall remain in force and have the same effect as if this ordinance had not been passed.

Sent to referendum 6 May 1861 by the legislature, and approved by the voters by a vote of 104,471 to 47,183 on 8 June 1861

Missouri Secession Ordinance

An act declaring the political ties heretofore existing between the State of Missouri and the United States of America dissolved.

Whereas the Government of the United States, in the possession and under the control of a sectional party, has wantonly violated the compact originally made between said Government and the State of Missouri, by invading with hostile armies the soil of the State, attacking and making prisoners the militia while legally assembled under the State laws, forcibly occupying the State capitol, and attempting through the instrumentality of domestic traitors to usurp the State government, seizing and destroying private property, and murdering with fiendish malignity peaceable citizens, men, women, and children, together with other acts of atrocity, indicating a deep-settled hostility toward the people of Missouri and their institutions; and

Whereas the present Administration of the Government of the United States has utterly ignored the Constitution, subverted the Government as constructed and intended by its makers, and established a despotic and arbitrary power instead thereof: Now, therefore,

Be it enacted by the general assembly of the State of Missouri, That all political ties of every character new existing between the Government of the United States of America and the people and government of the State of Missouri are hereby dissolved, and the State of Missouri, resuming the sovereignty granted by compact to the said United States upon admission of said State into the Federal Union, does again take its place as a free and independent republic amongst the nations of the earth.

This act to take effect and be in force from and after its passage.

Approved by the Missouri Legislature on October 31, 1861.

Kentucky Secession Ordinance

Whereas, the Federal Constitution, which created the Government of the United States, was declared by the framers thereof to be the supreme law of the land, and was intended to limit and did expressly limit the powers of said Government to certain general specified purposes, and did expressly reserve to the States and people all other powers whatever, and the President and Congress have treated this supreme law of the Union with contempt and usurped to themselves the power to interfere with the rights and liberties of the States and the people against the expressed provisions of the Constitution, and have thus substituted for the highest forms of national liberty and constitutional government a central despotism founded upon the ignorant prejudices of the masses of Northern society, and instead of giving protection with the Constitution to the people of fifteen States of this Union have turned loose upon them the unrestrained and raging passions of mobs and fanatics, and because we now seek to hold our liberties, our property, our homes, and our families under the protection of the reserved powers of the States, have blockaded our ports, invaded our soil, and waged war upon our people for the purpose of subjugating us to their will; and

Whereas, our honor and our duty to posterity demand that we shall not relinquish our own liberty and shall not abandon the right of our descendants and the world to the inestimable blessings of constitutional government: Therefore,

Be it ordained, That we do hereby forever sever our connection with the Government of the United States, and in the name of the people we do hereby declare Kentucky to be a free and independent State, clothed with all power to fix her own destiny and to secure her own rights and liberties.

And whereas, the majority of the Legislature of Kentucky have violated their most solemn pledges made before the election, and deceived and betrayed the people; have abandoned the position of neutrality assumed by themselves and the people, and invited into the State the organized armies of Lincoln; have abdicated the Government in favor of a military despotism which they have placed around themselves, but cannot control, and have abandoned the duty of shielding the citizen with their protection; have thrown upon our people and the State the horrors and ravages of war, instead of attempting to preserve the peace, and have voted men and money for the war waged by the North for the destruction of our constitutional rights; have violated the expressed words of the constitution by borrowing five millions of money for the support of the war without a vote of the people; have permitted the arrest and imprisonment of our citizens, and transferred the constitutional prerogatives of the Executive to a military commission of partisans; have seen the writ of habeas corpus suspended without an effort for its preservation, and permitted our people to be driven in exile from their homes; have subjected our property to confiscation and our persons to confinement in the penitentiary as felons, because we may choose to take part in a cause for civil liberty and constitutional government against a sectional majority waging war against the people and institutions of fifteen independent States of the old Federal Union, and have done all these things deliberately against the warnings and vetoes of the Governor and the solemn remonstrance's of the minority in the Senate and House of Representatives: Therefore,

Be it further ordained, That the unconstitutional edicts of a factious majority of a Legislature thus false to their pledges, their honor, and their interests are not law, and that such a government is unworthy of the support of a brave and free people, and that we do therefore declare that the people are thereby absolved from all allegiance to said government, and that they have a right to establish any government which to them may seem best adapted to the preservation of their rights and liberties.

Adopted 20 Nov 1861, by a "Convention of the People of Kentucky"

###

About the Author

JERRY C. BREWER is a native Texan whose ancestors came from Wales during the American Colonial period, settling in North Carolina and Virginia. They later migrated to Tennessee, Alabama, Mississippi, Texas and Oklahoma. Many of those served honorably in Alabama, Texas, Mississippi and Virginia military units during the War Between The States.

The author graduated from the University of Oklahoma with a BA in Journalism. He has served as managing editor of a suburban Oklahoma City newspaper and published weekly newspapers in Chillicothe, Texas and Sentinel, Oklahoma. In addition to his newspaper work, he also worked in television and film production and taught both as an associate instructor at Oklahoma City University in the 1990s.

He has authored two other books, a family history entitled, "...Unto Thy People: The Story of Our Fathers," and "...Unto The Churches of Galatia: A Commentary on Paul's Epistle To The Galatians."

He has also been a gospel preacher for many years, preaching throughout the South and Southwest. He is married to the former Sherlene Holley of Carter, Oklahoma. They have six children, 17 grandchildren and two great grandchildren.

Available from Shotwell

Dixie Rising: Rules for Rebels by James R. Kennedy

Punished with Poverty: The Suffering South by James R. and Walter D. Kennedy

Annals of the Stupid Party: Republicans Before Trump by Clyde N. Wilson (The Wilson Files 3)

Nullification: Reclaiming Consent of the Governed by Clyde N. Wilson (The Wilson Files 2)

The Yankee Problem: An American Dilemma by Clyde N. Wilson (The Wilson Files 1)

Maryland, My Maryland: The Cultural Cleansing of a Small Southern State by Joyce Bennett

Washington's KKK: The Union League During Southern Reconstruction by John Chodes

When the Yankees Come: Former South Carolina Slaves Remember Sherman's Invasion. Edited with Introduction by Paul C. Graham

Southerner, Take Your Stand! by John Vinson

Lies My Teacher Told Me: The True History of the War for Southern Independence by Clyde N. Wilson (Available as a free eBook at www.FreeLiesBook.com)

Emancipation Hell: The Tragedy Wrought By Lincoln's Emancipation Proclamation by Kirkpatrick Sale

Southern Independence. Why War? - The War to Prevent Southern Independence by Dr. Charles T. Pace

GREEN ALTAR BOOKS (Literary Imprint):

A New England Romance & Other Southern Stories by Randall Ivey

Tiller (Clay Bank County, IV) by James Everett Kibler

Publisher's Note

IF YOU ENJOYED THIS BOOK or found it useful, interesting, or informative, we'd be very grateful if you would post a brief review of it on the retailer's website.

In the current political and cultural climate, it is important that we get accurate, Southern friendly material into the hands of our friends and neighbours. *Your support can really make a difference* in helping us unapologetically celebrate and defend our Southern heritage, culture, history, and home!

———

For more information, or to sign-up for notification of forthcoming titles, please visit us at

www.SHOTWELLPUBLISHING.com

Southern Without Apology.

www.ingramcontent.com/pod-product-compliance
Lightning Source LLC
Chambersburg PA
CBHW071712160426
43195CB00012B/1652